D0434933

POST-WAR BRITAIN

Post-War Britain

A BACKGROUND BOOK

C. M. Woodhouse

DUFOUR EDITIONS

CHESTER SPRINGS

PENNSYLVANIA

CONTENTS

═══════

Introduction

HAS THE British people lived through a turning-point of history in the last twenty years? Few of us who remember pre-war Britain would doubt it. Yet historic turning-points, though often announced, are rather rare. It is easy to attach too much importance to immediate events. Sometimes history comes to define a turning-point in terms of events which few people could have noticed at the time. Sometimes the real turning-point is not an event so much as a change of public mood brought about by events which have already happened. In the years since the Second World War there have been events of immense significance in British history. There have also been almost revolutionary changes in the public mood. Do these or any of them amount to a historic turning-point, and if so, when is it to be dated?

Such questions are peculiarly difficult to answer in the case of the British people because of the strong, indeed unbreakable thread of continuity which persists through all our changes. One of the theses of this book is that the thread of continuity has been stronger than the pressures for change in the last twenty years of British history. While structural change has been going on all over the world around us, the atmosphere of continuity has tended to insulate Britain from it—not indeed completely, but to the extent that our reactions have generally been belated, and our awareness that our national problems are themselves structural in character has tended to follow events rather than march with them or ahead of them. Thus our historic turning-point, if there has been one, has to be identified in terms not so much of dramatic events as of public moods; though this of course is not to say that there have been no such events or that they have passed unnoticed.

Dramatic events have a strange habit of coinciding. The rising against the Russians in Budapest and the Anglo-French expedition against Egypt in 1956 provide a classic instance, though one in which it is not yet certain—and perhaps never

7

will be—whether there was a causal connection or merely a coincidence. Two other remarkable instances occurred in the particular years in which the first two post-war Labour governments came to power in Britain.

In 1945 their election coincided with the end of the Second World War and the beginning of the nuclear age. (For those who believe that history is not simply the record of political events, it may be added that August 1945, the month of the first atomic bomb, also saw the first publication of George Orwell's *Animal Farm*; and in the same summer the British public saw and heard the first operatic masterpiece by a British composer for many generations, Benjamin Britten's *Peter Grimes*.)

In 1964 the return to power of the Labour Party occurred within twenty-four hours of the fall of Khrushchev in the Soviet Union and the explosion of Communist China's first nuclear weapon.

It is natural to suppose, when confronted with such spectacular coincidences of immense events, that here is a turning-point in history, a watershed after which a new era begins. Obviously such events are of great importance, particularly in the field of technology. It is not easy to assess them on first impact. There is a temptation today to overestimate them just because they used once to be underestimated or even overlooked altogether. Before the nuclear revolution, the most important technological event of the twentieth century was the first flight of the aeroplane in December 1903. Yet the initial impact of that achievement was very small. Few people heard of it at the time, and some who heard of it disbelieved it. One looks in vain for any reference to manned flight in the *Annual Register* for 1903, or indeed for any of the next few years thereafter. It passes unrecorded in the last volume of the original edition of the *Cambridge Modern History*, published in 1910.

Today, however, public reaction to such events is instantaneous; no scientific claim is too improbable to be accepted; and the assumption that we are on or over the threshold of a new epoch in human history is universal and virtually unchallenged.

8

So it was for most people in 1945; so it was for some—rather fewer—again in 1964. Yet looking back over the last twenty years one finds at first a stronger impression of continuity than of revolutionary change after 1945, and the same looked like being true in 1966. Change came to Britain, of course, in the first two decades after the Second World War; change is no doubt in progress again. But it was and is a less immediate and revolutionary process than appeared at first sight.

It is the purpose of this book to examine the process so far as the British people and their political leaders are concerned. It is a story partly of successful adjustment and partly of mal-adjustment. The balance of success to maladjustment is on the whole more favourable in domestic affairs and less favourable in external relations. But neither scene presents a record either of total success or of total failure.

The reason in both cases lies in the discrepancy between the rate of change in events outside the British people's control and the rate of change in our realisation of what was happening to us. Sometimes the discrepancy was great, sometimes narrow, but it was always there. The period when it was narrowest was perhaps the twelve months between the Suez Canal crisis and the launching of the first Soviet *sputnik* (1956–57). Perhaps 1965 may deserve to be recorded as another such year, though at present it seems unlikely. Each of these two years coincided with the first year in office of a Prime Minister peculiarly sensi-tive to the 'wind of change' blowing across the landscape of the world. But this was conspicuously not the case during the first decade after the Second World War. What is striking about the years which followed the election of the first Labour govern-ment ever to enjoy a large majority is the evidence of continuity with the past rather than the arrival of a new age. This is the unavoidable theme of the chapters that follow.

I

The Land of Dreams

━━━

THERE WERE two surprises about the accession to power of the Labour Party in 1945, neither of which ought in fact to have been surprising. One was that they won the election at all, let alone with such a massive majority; the other was that they proved not, after all, to be a party of revolution.

The latter surprise was more deeply felt abroad—in Europe and America, and perhaps to a lesser extent in the Soviet Union and the dependencies of what was still called the British Empire —than it was among the British people themselves, who had seen the Labour leaders in office during five years of national coalition. But the surprise at the extent of the swing to Labour was felt hardly less deeply at home than abroad, even among those who had voted Labour. There were virtually no psephologists in those days to tell us what we were collectively thinking. What would they have told us in June 1945 if there had been?

Although no answer can be anything but speculative, some speculations are probable. It is doubtful whether more than a sophisticated minority of voters was thinking in terms of the Conservative Party's pre-war record or of the contrast between Churchill's merits as a leader in war and peace. The underlying motive was perhaps an instinctive feeling that since Britain was committed by common consent to a new kind of society—the Welfare State—in which the scope of government action must be substantially extended at the expense of private initiative, it was preferable that such a society should be inaugurated under the aegis of a party which was known to believe in it rather than one which was still doubtful about it. That would have been a fair assessment of political attitudes at the time. Yet the fact is that the commitment was indeed a matter of common consent, and that a large and irreversible measure of progress towards it had already been made under the Coalition government before it broke up. That is one reason for the impression of continuity before and after June 1945.

It was a continuity which went back well before the Second World War. Not only Lloyd George, but Neville Chamberlain, was among the architects of the Welfare State. Many of the social phenomena which so impressed and sometimes depressed post-war moralists—the decline of the Churches' influence, the relaxation of sexual morality, the increase of drink and gambling, the proliferation of dangerous motor-cars—had their roots in the nineteen-twenties and thirties, their growth being at best temporarily stunted, and in some cases even accelerated, by the war.

The war itself was responsible, of course, for a vast expansion of state-directed activity. But much of it could not be directly related to the fighting of the war, unless on the assumption that the war was to last for a generation or more. Much of it owed its inspiration to Beveridge's *Report on Social Insurance and Allied Services* (1942), a seminal work which came to be treated, unfortunately in the long run, as virtually holy writ. Thanks to Beveridge, Keynes and a handful of other influential publicists, Britain was readier than most people realised for a strong dose of state management, whether theoretically socialist or not, in the last year of the war. However doubtful Conservatives might be about the chosen course, they were parties in the first half of 1945 to many measures which had little relation to the war effort. It would have been less surprising to find them in the programme of the subsequent Labour government than in the last stages of a preponderantly Conservative coalition; but there they were, and almost nobody objected.

A few brief examples will show that this is not merely a theoretical rationalisation. If one were to trace the record back to earlier years, the most prominent places would be occupied by the Education Act and the Town and Country Planning Act, both of 1944. But the trend is perhaps better indicated by less prominent examples falling within the last six months of coalition or caretaker government, when military victory was already certain and exigencies of war could not be seriously invoked.

Early in 1945, the Land and War Works Act altered in the government's favour the basis of compensation for compulsorily requisitioned land. Soon afterwards, the Distribution of Industry Act gave the government powers to regulate the location of industry in peace-time. In March 1945 the formation of three national air corporations was announced, with practically no reference to the future of private air-lines. Later in the same month the Reid Committee on the coal industry recommended a reorganisation entailing at least the regionalisation of the pits; and a few weeks later the Conservative 'caretaker' government accepted the recommendation, though it hoped that the reorganisation could be achieved voluntarily.

Again in March 1945, the government committed itself to a huge state-sponsored housing programme. At one time Churchill spoke of half a million houses a year. The figure was eventually set at 220,000; but it is worth recollecting, as evidence of the essential continuity of policy, that in the late nineteen-thirties house-building had reached over 350,000 a year under the previous Conservative-dominated coalition, including over 75,000 Council houses.

To complete the list of measures taken by the Churchill governments (coalition or caretaker) before the General Election, they passed the Industrial Injuries Insurance Act and the Family Allowances Act in June; they created the Arts Council; and they took the first steps towards restoring self-government in Burma and extending it to India. Finally, the Conservative election manifesto no less than those of the Labour and Liberal parties contained an explicit commitment to full employment in the Beveridge sense. All these were straws in the wind of change. They fell a long way short of socialism, but they were equally a long way from the traditional conception (or misconception) of conservatism.

Not less significant of the trend was the attitude of leading Conservatives to planning. It is fashionable to represent them as belatedly converted to planning in the early nineteen-sixties, after resolutely opposing it in principle during the post-war Labour administrations. This is an over-simplification. From 1941 onwards, state planning had become a matter of habit to

13

Conservative Ministers as much as to Socialists. Nor were the lines between them rigidly drawn and doggedly defended in the last ditch on either side after 1945. In a debate on nationalisation in November 1946, Harold Macmillan conceded that 'some planning was necessary' and Stafford Cripps, by way of contrast, stated that controls were continually being re-examined with a view to removal.

A year later came the Conservatives' *Industrial Charter*, bearing the stamp of Butler's acute and humane intellect. Those who think of Winston Churchill, even, as simply an old-fashioned imperialist do so at the cost of forgetting his role in Asquith's administration some forty years earlier, besides ignoring the fact that he committed his party to maintaining full employment and the social services at every post-war election.

Looked at in retrospect, therefore, the General Election of 1945 did not present the country with two such diametrically opposite alternatives as many thought at the time. But given the choice between two mildly socialist programmes, it is not surprising that the electors chose the party which not only offered the stronger dose but also appeared to believe in it with more conviction. Nor is it surprising that after the election many things went on very much as before. The great revolution simply did not come about. A somewhat halting but not unsuccessful process of readjustment took place at home, so far as the government was able to determine the course of events. But abroad, where the government was much less able to determine the course of events, things were changing in a much more decisive way, to which the British public gave only spasmodic and uncomprehending attention.

During its first eighteen months, the Labour government enjoyed a comparative respite in foreign affairs while it got on with its domestic programme, in which the British public was much more interested. The respite was due partly to a reaction from the violence of war, partly to a failure to appreciate the long-term change which had taken place in Britain's material status, partly to the absence of immediate crises. There were problems in plenty building up—the future of the country's

14

overseas dependencies, beginning with India and Palestine; the breakdown of the war-time alliance with the Soviet Union; the adverse balance of payments and chronic shortage of dollars, aggravated by the sale of overseas investments to finance the war and by the US government's abrupt termination of Lease-Lend in August 1945; the utter devastation of vast areas of Europe and Asia—but these problems did not reach what the public would recognise as a crisis during the Labour government's honeymoon period up to the end of 1946.

Still less did the public appreciate that we were moving into an era in which a totally independent foreign policy was no longer possible for Britain. On the contrary, with the British Empire still nominally intact, we could reasonably claim equality with the two super-states, the USA and the Soviet Union, in a way which was not open to other European imperial or ex-imperial powers. The public was on the whole relieved to find that foreign policy underwent no revolutionary change under Attlee and Bevin. Only the left wing of the Labour Party was resentful at being deprived of a distinctively socialist foreign policy, thus showing that they too had failed to recognise the impossibility of any totally independent policy.

For the best part of two years, therefore, the government was scarcely harried at all by the opposition over its foreign policy, though some of its own nominal supporters (who looked to Professor Harold Laski for their intellectual inspiration) were a good deal less tolerant. Even in domestic policy the opposition was more selective and less comprehensive than had been expected. The extent and limitations of the underlying acceptance by Conservative opinion of the new trend in domestic policy—and indeed the limited degree to which the trend was new—can be judged from the record of opposition to particular measures.

The Labour election manifesto in 1945 had promised nationalisation of the Bank of England, fuel and power, inland transport, iron and steel; and also a system of controls over the economy and prices. Some Socialists criticised the lack of any promise to nationalise land or to control the selling price of houses. In November 1945 the government re-affirmed its nationalisation programme, specifying coal, electricity, gas, civil aviation, telecommunications, road and rail transport, and the docks, but not shipping. Even iron and steel were to be postponed to await a report commissioned by the Coalition government. Not all these measures were presented, nor were all ferociously opposed by the Conservatives or warmly welcomed by the Socialists.

Having been agreeably surprised by the mildness of Hugh Dalton's initial plans as Chancellor of the Exchequer, the opposition judged each step on its merits. During the first eighteen months, they offered little or no opposition to the Supplies and Services Act (which prolonged two-thirds of the war-time controls for five years), to the Bank of England Act (which hardly altered the reality of things anyway), to the legislation for agriculture (which did little more than give statutory effect to a system built up on war-time exigencies), to the National Insurance Act, the creation of the Atomic Energy Authority, the New Towns Act, the nationalisation of the Cable and Wireless Company, or the Exchange Control Act (except on the principle of making it permanent). What then did they oppose? The list is interesting.

They voted, for instance, against the Rent Control Act for furnished accommodation, the repeal of the Trades Disputes Act of 1927, the National Health Service Act (though not opposed to a state service in principle), the creation of a Control Board for the steel industry, the imposition of a fixed proportion in the housing programme of four Council houses to every one privately built, the Civic Restaurants Act, the Cotton Act; and of course against all the other nationalisation measures. Some of them (but only a minority) voted against the terms of the dollar loan from the USA and Canada at the end of 1945.

They attacked the government over the slow rate of demobilisation, over the hardships imposed on the domestic consumer by the export drive, and over the introduction of bread rationing in particular. No doubt with a consciousness of the public association of Conservatives with private monopolies, they also criticised the government for its excessive tolerance of over-powerful national institutions: for instance, they tried in vain to persuade the government to revise the charter of the BBC, and to frustrate the insistence of large Trade Unions (particularly the Transport and General Workers') on the 'closed shop'.

The upshot of such examples is that the Conservative Party did not refuse to accept a considerable extension of the power of the state; but they wished to draw the line of demarcation in a different place, and their criterion was respect for the rights and liberties of the individual. Such at least was the impression which they wished to create. It was consistent with the principle of continuity rather than revolution. But it did not convince the public. In two successive years (November 1945 and 1946) the local elections showed that the Labour Party still retained public confidence. Labour Party Conferences, though full of controversy, were ebullient and self-confident; Conservative Party Conferences were puzzled and gloomy.

The public mood was certainly not enthusiastic: general shortages (especially of bread, coal and houses) and Crippsian austerity saw to that. But discontent was only sporadic and ill-organised, taking the form of unauthorised 'squatting' in un-occupied premises or of ephemeral associations like the House-wives' League to demand more and better consumer goods. A sign of the times was the failure of the first attempt of the former British Union of Fascists (under the new name of the Vigilantes Action League) to exploit discontent by organising a mass meeting at the Albert Hall in March 1946. Only 200 people turned up, together with an equal number of Communists to prevent the meeting from taking place.

People had grievances, but they were not fundamentally pessimistic. Both their grievances and their optimism had the same underlying cause—the assumption that things had not really changed. There were many signs of exhaustion and even some of demoralisation. There was more stringent rationing than ever; there were 'spivs' flourishing on a black market; there was a crime wave, and the courts were congested with a great increase in divorce. There was also much idealism, which expressed itself in contributions to UNRRA, in expanding colonial development and in sending parcels of food to defeated

17

Germany. But our resources were over-taxed. 'Britain Can Make It' was a happy slogan which did not always correspond to reality. The air corporations were kept aloft by American aircraft, the cinemas kept open by American films; though in both cases government protection helped to keep the native industries alive.

The arts in Britain were deplorably stagnant. Music attracted great audiences, but little of it was original British work; and the motives of concert-goers were mainly escapist. The theatre flourished chiefly on revivals, thanks to a conjunction of superlative actors with a dearth of contemporary playwrights. (It is melancholy to record that the first post-war triumphs of British drama fell to Terence Rattigan and William Douglas-Home.) There was virtually no expansion of higher education: it was in every way characteristic that the first two post-war British universities were founded in West Africa and the West Indies. There was a deep nostalgia for the past and a tacit assumption that the world owed the British people a living as a reward for having stood alone. So far as the 'home front' was concerned, it was as if the war had not yet ended.

At the same time, however, there was a fundamental optimism based on the conviction that all these frustrations, all this weariness of the spirit, were only passing grievances. The sense of continuity fostered the belief that once the scars of war were healed, the good times would return. Britain was, it was assumed, still a great power, one of the Big Three. We still had our Empire: even in the Labour Party's statements of policy before and after the General Election of 1945, there was no hint of colonial independence. We were still in the forefront of science and technology. In 1945 people learned for the first time about radar, in 1946 about electronic computers—both pioneered in Britain. They already knew that British scientists led the world in developing the jet engine, the invention of penicillin and the discovery of atomic energy.

Industrial design was a cognate field in which British pre-eminence could be claimed, at least for the time being. It was on view in the exhibition at the Victoria and Albert Museum opened by the King in September 1946, and seen by a million and a half visitors by the end of the year. Londoners had a special sense of pride, having survived the blitz to become the scene of the first assembly of the United Nations and of innumerable other international gatherings. Even in international sport, which meant more than any of these things to most people, it was assumed that we were still at the summit. Nothing, in fact, had greatly changed. Such was the world of fantasy in which we lived for almost two years after the war.

2

The First Disillusionment

THE FIRST—but abortive—awakening of the British people from their day-dreams occurred with a series of shocks in 1947. Overseas, the simmering troubles of Palestine and India came to a head in concurrent crises which led in each case to an abrupt and premature withdrawal of the British government from its responsibilities. For rather different reasons, our responsibilities in Greece were ceded to the Americans under the Truman Doctrine. All three countries lapsed into internecine warfare which Britain in effect acknowledged its total impotence to control.

Other European powers—France, Italy and the Netherlands —had already given up substantial colonial possessions under international (including British) pressures. Britain herself had been slow to read the writing on the wall, even though some of it was written in her own hand. Our consequent humiliations were only partly redeemed by the good grace with which they were eventually faced as accomplished facts. But it was at home rather than overseas that the blows of 1947 were most acutely felt.

The year began in an atmosphere of cautious optimism, with considerable progress towards the achievement of two objectives: first, the passage of social legislation to benefit the working population (though Aneurin Bevin, the Minister of Health, was embroiled in a bitter argument with the British Medical Association about the proposed National Health Service); second, the reconstruction of the economy to eliminate Britain's foreign indebtedness. It was not yet generally realised to what an extent these two objectives might be in conflict. The encouraging evidence was that the exports target for 1946 had been exceeded by some 20%, and that the number of days lost by strikes and stoppages in industry was minute compared with the first year after the First World War. In particular, coal production in 1946 was up by more than 6 million tons over 1945. Yet these were just the points at which the British economy proved most vulnerable in 1947. The two crucial disasters were the fuel crisis in February and the dollar crisis six months later.

Both were foreseeable, and indeed foreseen, but not by the general public. There had been warnings of a shortage of coal before the end of 1946. It was aggravated by the administrative upheaval accompanying nationalisation (vesting day being January 1, 1947) and by the coldest winter for more than half a century. But the crisis would probably have occurred in any case. It was not only economically but psychologically catastrophic. The closure of factories, the failure of light and heating at home, the rise of unemployment temporarily to more than two million, the literal necessity to carry coals to Newcastle—all this was bad enough to remain long in the public memory.

Yet almost worse was to follow when a glorious summer succeeded the winter of our discontent. One of the consequences of the dollar loan from the USA and Canada in 1946 was the imposition of free convertibility on sterling in 1947. By July it was clear that the demand could not be met, and in August convertibility was suspended. This further humiliation cut off the British people from many pleasures and luxuries such as tobacco, petrol, newsprint, films and travel abroad. It also taught them, in a hazy and ill-assimilated fashion, that London was no longer the economic and financial capital of the world.

Not only were we now proved to be unable to impose our will abroad: we were unable even to manage our own domestic economy, or even to produce enough of the only major industrial raw material in which we had always been self-sufficient, namely coal. All these troubles were invisibly inter-connected. Ernest Bevin used often to say: 'Give me so many million tons of coal, and I will save Europe from Communism.' The fact that we could no longer export coal not only reduced our capacity to help devastated Europe, it also added to the chronic

21

burden of our balance of payments. So did the vast sterling balances accumulated by foreign countries, particularly India and Egypt, during the war. So did the sale of our foreign investments, particularly dollar securities to pay for the war. Unable to pay our way even on current account, we could not sustain the heavy commitment of our armed forces in Germany, Greece, Palestine and India.

These facts were too remote, however, for the man in the street. And although he had shown himself in 1940 perfectly capable of grasping and grappling with harsh facts, when they presented themselves (or were presented) to him in comprehensible form, in 1947–48 they were not so presented. Rather, they were masked by policy and circumstance.

The unparalleled winter gave the government what is loosely known as an 'alibi' for the fuel crisis. The Marshall Plan, announced by the US Secretary of State in June 1947, offered the prospect of relief from the dollar crisis. The US government also took over, mercifully without mutual recriminations, most of Britain's financial commitments in Greece and the dollar-component of our expenditure on the British zone in Germany. Although the generosity of the Americans' reactions was acknowledged by all political leaders in Britain, it did not prevent the gradual rising of a tide of anti-Americanism at the level of public opinion.

There were some elements of justification in this sentiment. The USA had, in fact, helped to precipitate the dollar crisis by the abrupt termination of Lease-Lend and the unrealistic terms of the 1946 loan. Both Presidents Roosevelt and Truman had aggravated Britain's colonial problems—the former by his deference to Stalin as a companion 'anti-imperialist', the latter by his electioneering gambit of pressing Britain to admit another 100,000 Jews into Palestine. But although there were real grounds for resentment, the basis of popular anti-Americanism was more probably a growing awareness that the USA had taken Britain's place as a great power.

The effect of the setbacks of 1947 was therefore a feeling that the British people had suffered an unmerited injustice rather than that they must adjust themselves and pull their socks up.

It was perhaps, in the long run, unfortunate that the more serious consequences were averted by an external rescue operation. Marshall Aid alone saved Britain from an unemployment level of a million and a half in 1948, as Aneurin Bevan frankly admitted. But the British public hardly took the fact in. This was not surprising when it is recalled that at the same time the Labour government was pressing on with an extensive programme of nationalisation—electricity, gas, transport and eventually steel were the main items of 1947–49—from which there was no obvious reason to expect any increase of production and wealth, whatever might be said for them in terms of social responsibility and equitable distribution. Experience suggested rather the contrary—particularly in the coal industry, where strikes and absenteeism were greatly increasing, and no measurable profit was shown until the tenth year after nationalisation (1956–57).

Although the British people were beginning to be disenchanted with their Labour government, it was in general without fathoming the inescapable reality. The reality could be seen in statistics which were meaningful only to those prepared to compare and interpret them over a period of years: for example, the balance of payments, which showed a deficit of £230 million in 1946 rising to £381 million in 1947, and a small surplus of £26 million in 1948 thanks only to Marshall Aid; or the gold reserves, which fell at the end of three successive years from £664 million (1946) to £512 million (1947) and to £457 million (1948). The government's policy of low interest and high taxation, used to expand the social services rather than industrial production, created inflationary pressures internally and contributed nothing to the improvement of exports.

The paradoxical situation was neatly summarised by Lord Samuel speaking in the House of Lords early in 1948, when he pointed out that the nation was £700 million to the good on domestic budget and £700 million to the bad on overseas account. Nor was the budget surplus productively applied. The National Health Service absorbed far more than was estimated: housing, roads, schools and universities all suffered cuts in investment. The effect of inflation was most sharply

23

felt by pensioners, whose benefits increased at a much lower rate than the rise in the cost of living.

The learned weeklies and dailies withdrew their support or tolerance from the government before the end of 1947. The world of business and industry did so earlier, but was slower to show it bluntly. The employers' organisations co-operated with Cripps and the Trade Union leadership in setting up productivity councils; they read the government mild lectures against nationalisation, especially of steel; but it was not until late in 1949 that their impatience broke out in forceful forms, like the interruptions of a speech by Prime Minister Attlee at the Lord Mayor's banquet.

The opposition in Parliament was not far ahead of the public in its understanding of the national malaise. It fought furiously against nationalisation, and it denounced as tyranny the government's inevitable reactions, such as the imposition of a fixed time-table (the 'guillotine') for the first time ever on the Committee stage of legislation, or the bitterly contested amendment of the Parliament Act to ensure the passage of the Bill nationalising the steel industry. Hindsight leaves a melancholy impression of irrelevance in Parliament during these historic years; and that impression correctly reflects the public mood.

The public was not, on the whole, depressed by the diminution of Britain's status in the world. The withdrawal from overseas possessions was psychologically well managed. Sir John Seeley's famous phrase about 'a fit of absence of mind' still applied, as it generally had. To quit Palestine and India, which promptly did us the credit of collapsing into bloodshed and violence, was a positive relief to all except perhaps Churchill, who was temporarily (as often before) regarded as out of date. The public did not attempt to judge whether the consequences, such as the loss of political power in the Middle East or the weakening of the links with Australia and New Zealand, were acceptable or even inevitable: they were simply not foreseen.

Much more intelligible to the man in the street was the rising threat from the Soviet Union, which led to the Brussels Treaty in 1948 and the North Atlantic Treaty in 1949. Stalin represented a danger of a familiar kind, to which the British people knew how to react. It was a danger, however, which they did not yet fully appreciate that they could never again face alone, but only as a junior partner with the USA. So far as foreign affairs were concerned, the reasons why the public did not seriously lose confidence in the government were a combination of indifference, incomprehension and national obstinacy.

It was different at home. It was characteristically in the local elections that the first substantial signs of discontent emerged, first in November 1947, and again more dramatically (especially in London) in April 1949. The British people had not reconciled themselves to the new state of affairs at home as they had at least acquiesced in it abroad. They did not see why shortages and austerity and wage restraint should continue three or four years after the war. They did not understand why sterling had to be devalued in September 1949, though they recognised it as a national humiliation. They suspected that the Socialists, especially Cripps, enjoyed restrictions for their own sakes. Such of them as might read it would have found their heresies confirmed by a little book called *Are These Hardships Really Necessary?* by the eminent Keynesian economist, Roy Harrod. But the public was cheered or depressed by simpler things: cheered by Princess Elizabeth's wedding in 1947, or the New Look in women's clothes in 1948–49; depressed by Britain's poor showing in the first Olympic Games since the war, and against the first Australian cricket team on tour, both in 1948. Such things were taken to be the true portents of Britain's standing in the world. They relieved or darkened the stark reality of having too few homes, too little coal and meat, too frequent strikes, too many emergencies in the public services. The Trade Unions began for the first time to be looked on as enemies of society rather than protectors of the working class—a psychological transition of the first importance.

The government and Parliament carried the blame, rightly or wrongly. It is significant of the secular change through which Britain's history was passing that discontent extended to the leadership of the opposition as well as the government. Conservative Party conferences in this period were no less torn by criticism than those of the Labour Party. At the latter it was

25

chiefly defence and foreign policy which came under attack from the left wing—for maintaining conscription, for supporting the USA against the Soviet Union, for allowing Germany to be resurrected on Marshall Aid, for spending too much on armaments at the expense of the social services. Conservatives criticised their leaders for acquiescing too readily in Socialist policies, for failing to speak up for the British Empire, for having produced no clear and concise statement of policy. The superficial and irrelevant character of all these criticisms shows that what the malcontents were really criticising was the world they were living in, which they had not yet begun to understand.

The political leaders were in fact much more alive to the realities of the country's problems than their followers, unfashionable though it is to admit it. On both sides of the House of Commons were men fully worthy of the traditions they had inherited: Attlee, Cripps, Bevin, Morrison, Bevan on the one side; Churchill, Eden, Stanley, Butler on the other. In retrospect it is clearly absurd to accuse them of having lacked understanding of the nation's problems: what they lacked was the means and resources for tackling them, and these were to be lacked by all future leaders of the British people so long as Britain remained an independent nation-state.

Independence of the traditional kind had been possible in the nineteenth century to a country with the size, population and resources of Britain, which were then all exactly right. In the twentieth century such independence was in the nature of things denied to a country of fifty million people, crowded on to an island which could not feed more than half of them, which had no raw materials of any significance except coal, and which was indefensible against modern armaments. It is understandable that the British people failed to grasp this fact in the aftermath of victory, but it cannot be held against their leaders that they too failed to see the problem. What they failed to agree about was the solution.

One solution, which was tried, was to continue to assert a great-power status against all the odds. The government declined to contract out of the fields of advanced technology which naturally identified a great power. They provided state support for the aircraft industry, and were rewarded with a close and not unsuccessful competition against the USA: both countries had supersonic aircraft flying in 1948, both put transatlantic jet services into operation in 1951. They set out to catch up with the USA and the Soviet Union in the development of atomic energy, and actually outdistanced both in the application of atomic reactors to produce electricity.

There were both credits and debits in the account. Against the brilliant successes pioneered by British scientists in the development of antibiotics, synthetic fibres, aviation and nuclear energy, must be set the abortive claims for cortisone, the catastrophe of the Comet 1, the disappointment over the Zeta reactor. The successes and failures increasingly had certain features in common. Only governments could afford to make decisions on the scale required; and international rivalry led to hastily taken risks and premature claims.

But in the case of Britain, there was another hazard, less generally realised. Being no longer large or rich enough to afford every kind of research and development that might be desired, we had to make difficult and irrevocable choices. Miscalculations were inevitable—among them, the failure to exploit the electronic computer commercially in good time, and the decision (belatedly reversed a few years later) to drop out of the competition in rocket-propulsion and space-satellites.

At the same time both government and opposition tried to evolve long-term plans for adjusting Britain's position in a world no longer tailor-made to suit a nation of our size. The basic question was: how was a nation of fifty millions to live on equal terms with nations three or four times as large, such as the USA or the Soviet Union? The answer presumably lay either in Europe or the Commonwealth. Political leaders on both sides consistently accepted the alternative diagnosis, but swayed between the one alternative and the other, hoping to achieve the best of both worlds. Churchill still insisted on the future of the British Empire, but he also set up the United Europe Committee early in 1947. Bevin and Eden openly agreed that the advent of the atomic bomb made some abatement of national sovereignty inevitable, though their backbenchers heard them say so in silence. Marshall Aid was intended to give an impetus towards the political unification of Europe, and both Attlee and Bevin accepted it in that spirit; but the more doctrinaire socialists in their party tenaciously resisted the intention, partly because of its American origin and partly because the other European countries were insufficiently socialist. Consequently when the Schuman Plan to create a European Coal and Steel Community was launched in May 1950, the Labour Party was caught in disarray. Even the Conservative welcome for it was later proved to be delusive, if not hypocritical.

The notion that the Commonwealth could provide Britain with an alternative stage on which to play a leading role again, though outdated in reality, still died hard. Britain, the Dominions and the Colonies were increasingly unnatural partners in trade as the latter progressed economically. Not only did their interests diverge, but Britain was prevented by international pressures from protecting the interests of her former dependencies when she wished to do so, as witness the resentment of Australia and New Zealand at the General Agreement on Tariffs and Trade in 1947. A broadening conception of the future role of the Commonwealth was admirable, but not enough by itself. Sometimes resources were insufficient, as they were for the Colonial Development Corporation; sometimes hasty miscalculations were to blame, as in the fiasco of trying to grow groundnuts in East Africa.

The most imaginative venture involving both the developed and the under-developed Commonwealth was Bevin's Colombo Plan in 1950. But that included countries outside the Commonwealth as well, thus emphasising the fact that there was no context in which the Commonwealth formed a natural, unique, comprehensive and exclusive unit.

Looked at without sentimentality about kinship and natural loyalties, the world had become a harsh place for the British people to live in. It was full of painful paradoxes to a people of generosity and good-will. The reconstruction of beaten enemies, in part at the expense of the British tax-payer, led to ruthless competition from Germany and Japan with some of Britain's staple industries, particularly ship-building. The readily accepted obligation of promoting the economic development of backward areas of the Commonwealth led to similar competition from India and Hong Kong with the cotton industry. The same obligation had an even more disquieting consequence in the long run: it was not the abject poverty of the past which led to the influx of immigrants from the West Indies and West Africa, and later from India and Pakistan, but the marginal improvement in their standard of living which enabled them to afford the journey for the first time. This result did not become apparent till the nineteen-fifties, but demographic problems in the age of full employment already exercised political leaders. Churchill forecast in 1948 a massive emigration of up to a quarter of the British population. Morrison foresaw, as early as mid-1946, that there would be difficulty in manning 'the dirty, unpleasant and often underpaid industries', and urged that we must make machines do the drudgery rather than cheap labour. The nineteen-sixties have underlined the forebodings of both.

The fact illustrated by both these expressions of anxiety was that, whatever place Britain might eventually occupy in the international perspective, survival and prosperity would depend on a new attitude to life. What was needed could be seen either in material or in moral terms. In material terms the keyword was 'modernisation'—a term later appropriated by all parties in the nineteen-sixties, but by no means an innovation. In moral terms the call was for regeneration, though far too often eminent churchmen put it in the merely negative form of denunciations of moral laxity. Both kinds of appeal found a meeting-point in the austere character of Stafford Cripps, who was equally assiduous in invoking Christian principles and in urging practical ideas upon industrialists and Trade Unionists.

The senior generation of Trade Union leaders ('more Methodist than Marxist', in Morrison's apt phrase) responded valiantly and not without success. At the first Trade Union Congress after the war, the President warmly advocated new attitudes now that Labour was in power: he spoke of modernisation, efficiency, productivity; he gave no blessing to the closed shop or to extravagant wage-claims; he criticised disruptive activities, which only a year or two later were to be identified more explicitly with the Communists. But far too many Trade Unionists of the middle ranks, particularly those in Parliament, could not forget the tribulations of the nineteen-thirties and never fully accepted that mass unemployment had gone for good.

Whether there were in the late nineteen-forties the beginnings of a regeneration of the British people's spirit and energies is hard to say. There were some favourable signs. In a material sense, life was already beginning to get better. Some rationing had ended; Harold Wilson at the Board of Trade started his 'bonfire of controls'; the trade balance was improving, and the dollar gap had nearly vanished, though admittedly this was mainly due to the devaluation of sterling in September 1949. In the industrial field, a notable symbol of the times was the name of Fawley on Southampton Water: here the first major oil refinery in Britain was opened in 1951, just in time to confront the Persian oil crisis, and it proved a model of well-planned industrial relations.

In the spiritual context it may be significant that the number of Anglican candidates for ordination reached its post-war peak in 1947, as did the number of communicants in 1950. Both figures later fell away, and then later rose again. There was even a reduction in the crime statistics, leading to the premature closure of some penal institutions in the early nineteen-fifties; but this trend also reversed itself in a few years.

The mood of the people, reflected as it generally is in its entertainments, was still escapist. The domination of television had begun, though still confined to the BBC. American films dominated the cinemas, and two American musical plays ran in London throughout the year 1948. The serious theatre meant either Shakespeare or the non-realist drama of Eliot, Fry, Bridie and Priestley. It was an advance on the purely post-prandial entertainment of the immediate post-war years, but it was a symptom of a transitory and uncertain mood. The coming shock of Arthur Miller, Brecht, and Tennessee Williams was felt as yet only in the esoteric clubs; and the 'angry young men' were still unheard-of by their infantile predecessors, the 'teddy-boys'. Though conscious of the need to face a very different future, the British people were still looking over their shoulder at the past.

It was in this mood that they hesitantly re-elected the Labour government at the beginning of 1950 by a greatly reduced majority. The result accurately reflected an attitude of total uncertainty. For the first time the real issue was the comparative competence of the two major parties as national managers, and there seemed to be little to choose. The choice was strongly, but not quite decisively, influenced for the first time by broadcasting. Here too the choice was complicated by the fact that the most compelling broadcaster on the Conservative side, Dr Charles Hill (once known as the 'Radio Doctor' and later as the master-mind of the British Medical Association's struggle with Aneurin Bevan), called himself a National Liberal.

Probably more decisive, though only marginally so, was the fear that Churchill would lead the country into a war against the Communist world in alliance with the United States. It came therefore as a considerable shock to the electors when that was precisely what the Labour government did, less than six months after its re-election.

The outbreak of the Korean War at the end of June 1950 is the principal reason why it is impossible to say whether or not a regeneration of the British people and a redirection of their energies were taking place in the last years of the Labour government; for the war undid much of the good work, and obliterated most of the mistakes of the preceding five years.

3

Return to Dreamland

THE KOREAN WAR proved far more disruptive to the British
economy than to the American, even though our stake in men
and resources was much smaller. In the USA there was still a
large margin of unemployment to be absorbed in the war effort;
in Britain, with full employment, there was none. The USA
was also more nearly self-sufficient than Britain in raw materials,
whose prices rose sharply as a result of the war. The effect on
our balance of payments in 1951 was catastrophic. Moreover,
civil and military needs were in competition for the same
scarce resources in materials and skilled man-power.

The time had not yet come, as it was to do with the transition
to missile and nuclear warfare, when the technology of civil and
military research, development and production was complementary and inter-connected, each contributing to advances in
the other and all sharing a common load of overheads. To
Britain the Korean War was a severe economic setback, promoting inflation and delaying the progress of the welfare state.
It was for these reasons that Aneurin Bevan and Harold Wilson
resigned from Attlee's government early in 1951.

Inevitably the war also destroyed, or at least postponed, the
hesitant interest which the British people had begun to show in
economic partnership with Europe. Such interest as survived
lay rather in the context of defence than economic co-operation, for obvious reasons. It was also more keenly nurtured,
again understandably, by the opposition than the government.
Thus, when the Schuman Plan was published a few weeks
before the Korean War broke out it was greeted with some
enthusiasm by Conservative spokesmen, with little by Bevin
(who seems to have been taken by surprise), and with positive
hostility by the Labour Party's left wing. A few weeks after the

Korean outbreak, Churchill made his famous speech at the Council of Europe, proposing a European Army under a European Minister of Defence. Good Europeans naturally assumed that a Conservative government would be more co-operative than the Socialists. But after Churchill returned to power in October 1951, the assumption was for a long time disappointed.

In view of the fairly wide consensus—one must not say unanimity—of informed opinion both before 1950 and after 1960 that a far-reaching merger of economic and political sovereignty with Europe represented the most logical and efficacious solution of Britain's post-war problems, it is interesting to examine why the impetus in that direction faltered and failed in the intervening decade. One clear reason is that the British people were not ready to accept it.

It is often argued (mostly by people who have no intention of charging themselves with political responsibility) that it is the duty of politicians to lead public opinion, not simply to follow it. This is true, provided only that the gap between the leaders and the led is not allowed to become too wide. Without endorsing the narrow doctrine of the electoral mandate, it is plain from the election statistics that the Conservative government of 1951 was no more called upon to pursue radical innovations than the Labour government of 1950. This would not have deterred Churchill if he had been personally determined to carry Britain into Europe. But it is also plain from the letter of his speeches, even before the 1951 General Election, that this was not his intention. Still less was it so when he examined the situation confronting him on his return to power.

The reasons are not at first sight so obvious. Since it was not characteristic of Churchill to use ambiguous language, and since it is certain that his language did mislead Europeans, they must have been complex reasons. There were, of course, the practical difficulties about a British partnership with Europe, which grew more familiar as the decade progressed. In particular, it was impossible without drastic modification to combine the British system of agricultural protection or that of Commonwealth preference with the systems of managing food-prices prevalent in Europe. But these were difficulties which only became fully relevant when the European movement had advanced a stage further, from the Coal and Steel Community to the full Economic Community or Common Market. There was reason to believe—and the belief was shared by the Commonwealth as well as Europe—that these difficulties were advanced by Britain in order to mask a deep-rooted reluctance to join Europe for other reasons.

One reason was no doubt distrust. It was doubted in Britain whether the Europeans really believed in their own movement towards unification. The European movement was defensive in origin. The purpose was to neutralise the German danger without keeping Germany permanently crushed and embittered. The Soviet threat made a restoration of Western Germany inevitable, though it was long resisted by the Attlee government and even longer by the French. In the words of a witty Frenchman, what was needed was a Germany strong enough to frighten the Russians but weak enough not to frighten the west Europeans. The European movement was designed to achieve this paradox. Schuman himself defined the purpose of the ECSC as being to make war between France and Germany impossible by inextricably linking their basic industries.

Associated with the plan was a project for internationalising the crucial area of the Saar, whose industrial wealth had been a source of Franco-German rivalry throughout the century. A further step in the same direction was the Pleven Plan for a European Army, launched in 1952. By 1954 many of these plans had collapsed. The Saar returned to Germany; the European Army was replaced by the compromise of Western European Union, involving virtually no sacrifice of national sovereignty. All these events seemed to justify British scepticism about the European movement. It was to prove mistaken, but it was decisive at the time.

A contributory factor was the diminution of the fear of war with the Soviet Union. The physical threat to Europe was probably always over-estimated. It helped to provide an impetus towards the unification of Europe, and was perhaps deliberately exaggerated for that purpose. But during the first

34

years of Churchill's post-war government (1951–53), it was clearly waning. The Korean War reached a deadlock in 1951, out of which a negotiated settlement was bound to follow sooner or later. The threat of Soviet expansion in Europe had been virtually extinguished with the success of the allied air-lift to break the Berlin blockade, the unpunished defiance of Stalin by Tito in Yugoslavia, and the defeat of the Communist rebellion in Greece. The death of Stalin in March 1953 marked the end of a troubled and threatening era.

Two months later, Churchill was able to propose a meeting of the great powers 'at the summit' which, although it took another two years to convene, encouraged the belief that the cold war was drawing to its close. Again, the belief may have been mistaken, but the fact that it was widely held was sufficient to withdraw the impetus of fear from Britain's relations with the continent of Europe.

The same years were troubled in a quite different way, for which a connection with Europe could provide no relief. The partial retreat from imperial power under the Labour government had whetted the appetite of self-styled nationalists all over the world to push the process further. The British government was faced in these years with simultaneous or immediately successive crises all over the world: in Malaya, Egypt, Iran, Kenya, British Guiana, Iraq, Cyprus, Jordan. Not all of these were colonial dependencies, and not all involved the use of force. But all had in common the desire to eliminate all forms of political, military or economic control by foreigners, especially Europeans. Britain was the principal target under attack, though France also had her share, first in South-East Asia and then in Africa.

It was a crisis which each colonial power had to face alone. The United States was at best lukewarm, at worst sanctimoniously critical. There was no solidarity between the European powers themselves: some were even making plans to inherit the economic position of their allies as they were forced out—the Germans and Italians in Iran and Egypt, for instance. The anti-colonialist movement had not yet consolidated into the so-called Afro-Asian bloc, which was to produce after 1955 a new European solidarity by way of reaction. In the years when the world crisis shifted away from relations with the Soviet Union to relations with the colonial and dependent territories, Britain stood peculiarly alone.

Independence of action was thus to some extent forced on the British government in the early nineteen-fifties. It also suited the mood of the time. The return of a Conservative government in 1951 was a last opportunity to prove that Britain could still stand alone and prosper in peace as in war. Standing alone was a favourite occupation of the British people. It was easily forgotten how short was the period when we did so in the Second World War, and how impossible it would have been to do so for much longer. The same instinct, with the same element of self-deception, persuaded the British people to give Churchill a last opportunity to do what the Socialists had failed to do: to make Britain again a great, prosperous and independent power. This did not mean severing alliances or breaking associations, but maintaining them on a strictly businesslike basis to enhance British interests and not allowing them to be used to push Britain around. This necessarily meant some retreat from the Conservatives' past declarations of interest in Europe, because it was clear that partnership with Europe, unlike the Commonwealth and the USA, must involve some diminution of sovereignty. Before accepting that price, Britain wanted to make sure whether or not she had a prosperous and secure future on the traditional basis of an independent nation-state.

For some years after 1951, it looked as if the answer was favourable. The clouds over the economy dispersed with remarkable rapidity. Expert pessimists like the leader-writers of financial journals were confounded by the success with which 'Tory freedom' appeared to work, and were reduced to complaining that the process was not being carried far or fast enough. Early in 1952 the *Economist* remarked doubtfully on the current *Economic Survey* that 'Ministers are not clear in their own minds what economic planning under a Conserva-Government involves.' By the end of the year the same journal described the economic improvement as 'a triumph for the financial policy of the government'. All the principal indicators were favourable, and continued so for several years.

In the decade from 1950 to 1959 the balance of payments on current account was consistently in surplus apart from two years which were exceptional for known reasons—1951 and 1955 (both, incidentally, election years, which are notoriously unfavourable to economic confidence). All rationing and most controls were eliminated by the end of 1954. The target of 300,000 houses a year was achieved in 1953. Employment remained at a high and stable level; the fear that the Conservatives would liquidate the welfare state proved unreal; and the fear of war also receded. In 1953 for the first time since the war an odd-numbered year passed without an economic crisis. All these factors contributed to the contrast between the hesitant shift of opinion from left to right in 1950–51 and the steadily growing vote of confidence which re-elected the Conservative government in 1955 and 1959. Britain seemed to have found her feet again without the benefits or disadvantages of European entanglements.

The bases of reviving confidence were unfortunately unsound. The improvement in the balance of payments was due in part to the effects of devaluation in 1949, the transient benefits of which were not sufficiently exploited, and partly to a fortuitous improvement in the terms of trade, which stored up grave difficulties for the under-developed primary-producer countries and hence, at one remove, for all of us in the further future. Full employment and good labour relations were bought at the cost of weakness in resisting wage-claims, and hence creeping inflation. Colossal deficits were accumulated by the nationalised industries, particularly the railways, coal and BOAC. Declining industries, such as cotton, were expensively and mistakenly kept alive at the expense of their more up-to-date competitors. Vital public services, particularly education, continued to be stinted: this was the price on the one hand of the high priority given to housing, and on the other hand of the defence programme. Yet the defence programme itself was scaled down well before the end of the Korean War on the ground that the burden was becoming, in Churchill's words, 'utterly beyond our economic capacity to bear'. Scaling down the defence programme became a regular exercise in the nineteen-fifties and sixties, a fact which is itself an ominous comment on the myth of complete national independence.

The defence programme is so crucial a matter that it makes a convenient starting-point for an examination of the fundamental unsoundness of the British position. In the age of conventional warfare, and even of atomic warfare so long as bombers could deliver warheads through existing defences, it remained possible for a nation of Britain's size and resources to claim complete independence. This possibility had long since eluded the grasp of small nations, and it was all too slowly realised that the same fate was about to overtake Britain. As guided missiles succeeded bombers, H-bombs succeeded earlier weapons, and a new generation of aircraft superseded even the early jets, two characteristics of the new era began to emerge. One was that military and civil technology were no longer simply competitive but also complementary, so that to contract out of the one would mean in the long run also contracting out of the other. The second was that a country of Britain's size and resources, single-handed, could neither generate the capital nor provide the market necessary for a completely independent modern technology, on which a completely independent foreign policy must rest. The failure to perceive these facts was the great delusion of Britain during most of the nineteen-fifties, just as it was of France under President de Gaulle in the nineteen-sixties.

Although the facts of twentieth-century life must have become apparent to British Ministers well before the end of the nineteen-fifties, they were too sophisticated for the general public. So long as Churchill remained Prime Minister, a natural instinct to resist them prevailed. The superficial indications of success were sufficient to consolidate public confidence for more than a decade. Many of the indications were not merely superficial but irrelevant and trivial. The public drew its sense of well-being not only from the undoubted improvement in its standard of living but from merely symbolic events such as the Festival of Britain on London's South Bank in

1951, or the simultaneous conquest of Everest and coronation of Queen Elizabeth II in 1953. It had a better right to be impressed by the successful test of the world's first atomic heating plant at Harwell in 1951, the explosion of the first British atomic bomb in 1952, and the growing success of British aircraft and aero-engines in the world's export markets.

At the same time there were many disappointments to remind the British people that they were no longer in the front rank of great powers. An American admiral was appointed, against passionate opposition by Churchill, to command NATO forces in the Atlantic; Britain was omitted, again against her will, from the ANZUS pact between Australia, New Zealand and the USA for the defence of the south-western Pacific area; and even in the Middle East, the historic area of British influence, a large measure of American political and economic infiltration was the price of bringing the Iranian and Egyptian crises to a temporary conclusion in 1954.

If British public opinion failed to be deeply stirred by these signs of reduced circumstances, it was because the mood of the time was inward-looking and nostalgic rather than extrovert and forward-looking. The Festival of Britain, with its deliberate echoes of 1851, was typical of this mood: although it was intended to project a modern image of Britain, it was little more than an image of 1851 brought up-to-date.

In the civilised arts a better case could be made for claiming that Britain had a future than in modern technology. British opera became a musical phenomenon of international importance in 1951, with seven new works by British composers; the British ballet based on Sadlers' Wells and Covent Garden conquered the USA and many other countries abroad, including eventually the Soviet Union itself; and the transatlantic theatrical exchange began to be a two-way traffic instead of simply a movement from New York to London.

Yet it must be admitted with regret that the cultural events of greatest significance in these years were the decision to create an Independent Television Authority in 1953 and the commencement of seemingly interminable theatrical runs like *The Mousetrap* and the Whitehall farces. This sort of thing was unquestionably what the British people really wanted. For them, what some hopefully called 'the New Elizabethan Age' had not begun. Nor did they much want it to begin.

4

The Crucial Years

THE FIRST eighteen months after the war (1945–46) had been a period of honeymoon optimism. The next three and a half years (1947–50) were a period of disillusionment. To speak of disillusionment is not to imply despondency or frustration: these were in fact notably absent. The word is here used in a non-emotive sense to mean simply the dissipation of illusions, the revelation to the people of Britain that the post-war world was not going to be what they had imagined.

Their natural reaction was to change their government. If the Labour Party could not make the world conform to their wishes, perhaps the Conservatives could do so: at any rate, it was worth trying, if only by a very narrow margin and therefore without much conviction. There followed a period of three years (1951–53) in which it began to seem that the change was justified by results. But the matter could be put in another way. The illusions were restored and the people were sheltered from reality by deceptive and inflationary devices. The world only appeared to be remoulded nearer to our heart's desire. A second period of disillusionment was bound to follow.

It came in the succeeding years, 1954–56. It was not, like the first disillusion, a gradual process of creeping realisation. Things might have been easier if it had been. But it came instead with a sudden and overwhelming shock at the end of 1956, when Britain found herself—to her quite unjustified amazement—impotent to assert her will in an international crisis of the first magnitude. If the signs had been read aright, the affair loosely and inaccurately known as 'Suez' need not have had so devastating a climax. The climax, involving Eden's resignation and a national humiliation, was not so much a sudden downfall of British might as a belated recognition that the requisite might was no longer at Britain's disposal. Britain was seen at last to be unable to pursue a completely independent foreign policy. But that had been the case for years: all that was new was the discovery of it. In this respect the calamity of Suez may be compared to the devaluation of sterling in 1949, which was also not so much the emergence of a new situation as the recognition of a situation which had long since existed.

There was therefore evidently something deceptive about the three years (1954–56) leading up to the moment of disillusionment. The good times on which the Conservative government had been so warmly congratulated in the previous three years appeared to be continuing. Their precarious foundations were concealed. Although there was in no sense a deliberate act of deception, in looking at the reasons for it the personality of Anthony Eden is clearly important. The years 1954–56 were pre-eminently his years throughout. He became Prime Minister only half-way through the period, but he had been Churchill's political heir-presumptive for a long time, and Churchill's powers were visibly failing from the time of his stroke in mid-1953. Eden was unfortunately ill at the same time, and never fully recovered.

But his downfall in 1956 cannot be attributed wholly to ill-health. Nor can it be attributed wholly to lack of experience of the complete range of ministerial responsibility. It is true that he had never held office in a department concerned with home affairs. But in opposition he had been a front-bench spokesman on many domestic issues. He led the opposition, for instance, to the repeal of the Trades Disputes Act, to the nationalisation of coal, and to the government's food policy in 1946; and it was he who launched the slogan of 'a property-owning democracy' in 1947. In any case, the occasion of his downfall was exclusively a matter of foreign policy, in which his experience or inexperience of domestic affairs was beside the point.

The significant point about Eden is that temperamentally he belonged to the past. For just that reason, he was an appropriate symbol of the short period in which he led the British people: he represented their mood, just as Churchill did that of 1940. To be a reactionary in this sense was not ignoble. It

42

had even its romantic and dramatic elements. But it was not the right mood for modernising Britain.

Even in Eden's special field of foreign policy, his techniques were those of an earlier age. He sought to apply traditional diplomacy even to such declared revolutionaries as Musaddiq, Nasser and Khrushchev, only to find that they did not respond in kind. Confronted with the collapse of the European Defence Community, he salvaged out of it Western European Union; he built the South-East Asia Treaty Organisation on the ruins of the French Union of Indo-China after the disaster of Dien Bien Phu; he created the Baghdad Pact on the trembling foundations of Middle East nationalism. All these structures were orthodox alliances of a traditional kind, typical of balance-of-power politics. But a balance of power was mathematically impossible in the nuclear age, when two powers so out-distanced the rest that no combination of lesser powers could equal either of them.

A similar verdict of trying to solve twentieth-century problems with nineteenth-century methods could be brought against another well-meaning policy of the day—that of amalgamating ex-colonies into federations as a condition of independence. In whose mind this policy originated it is hard to say, but it was inaugurated in the Central African Federation during the period when British external policy was largely guided by Eden. It was a policy which made sense only on the assumption that nationalism did not matter, or at any rate mattered a great deal less than economic advantage and administrative tidiness. Failure after failure was insufficient to eradicate this pious hope from the mind of British politicians, as federation after federation was abortively established: Central Africa (1953), the West Indies (1956), South Arabia (1959), Nigeria (1960), Malaysia (1963).

It was a device which appealed to the British mind. It was characteristic of the mood of the British political leadership of the day, which was well-intentioned, humane, and willing to move with the times, but largely unaware of the direction and speed of their movement. They had already moved past the point at which it was possible for a British government to

43

intervene or assert its will decisively overseas without the support of other and stronger powers. The rebellion in Cyprus (1955), the dismissal of General Glubb from Jordan (1956) and the successful defiance of Britain and France by President Nasser all taught the same lesson. Yet it was characteristic also of the British people at the time that the government's popularity conspicuously rose in the public opinion polls after the calamity of Suez.

British public opinion moves in paradoxical ways. Given that a leader of Eden's skill and experience was unable to control events in the field of foreign policy, the inevitable and correct inference was that they were beyond control by a power of Britain's magnitude. A different inference was in fact drawn. It was not that the necessary power did not exist, but that for some unexplained reason—perhaps ill-health, perhaps the treachery of colleagues, perhaps the long shadow of Churchill —Eden was simply not tough enough to exercise the power. Such a rumour had even been current at the beginning of 1956, when Eden had had to take the unprecedented step of denying that he was about to resign.

Yet in some respects there were valid reasons why the British public could reject the notion of having sunk to second-class status, and could cling to the delusion of being back among the great powers. The reasons lay in tangible evidence of expansion, modernisation and prosperity at home. Eden's brief spell at the top coincided with a turning-point in Britain's post-war evolution at home as well as abroad. The turn taken at home was in a different direction; and it is part of the paradox of Eden's last years in office that they coincided with disastrous setbacks abroad, where he was so expert, and with a new era at home, where he was reputed to be so much less at home himself.

These were the years in which R. A. Butler, as Chancellor of the Exchequer, declared to the Conservative Party Conference in October 1954 that it was possible to double the British people's standard of living in 25 years, 'if we run our policy properly and soundly'. A year later the same Chancellor had to introduce an autumn budget to rectify the miscalculations of his April budget, which immediately preceded a General Election. But although this underlined the conditional nature of his hypothesis, it did not invalidate his forecast. It proved to be a true forecast over the next ten years, granted the premiss and the necessary extrapolation.

But it was also true, as was pointed out by the next Chancellor, Harold Macmillan, in 1956 that since the war we had increased production by 25% and paid ourselves 80% extra for doing so. The rate of increase of wages had seldom accelerated so steeply as in these years. Over-full employment deprived employers of any power or incentive to resist exorbitant claims from the Trade Unions, which were simply passed on to the consumer in higher prices. The consequence was not merely inflation, but also a new social problem. Gaps in the labour force, when they occurred, were filled by a massive influx of immigrants from the Commonwealth, mostly (apart from the Irish) of non-European racial origins. The tide was not yet noticeable, but it was beginning to swell to a flood. In 1953 only 2,000 West Indians entered Britain; by 1960 the figure was 50,000; and even then the seemingly inexhaustible tide from India and Pakistan was only just beginning. British prosperity was thus being built on economic and social foundations which were still hidden from the increasingly easy-going and complacent people of Britain.

Nevertheless the advances were real, and they were not confined to the material present. Both the achievements and the plans of the early nineteen-fifties pointed to impressive prospects for the future, provided that the foundations were not washed away. Among the achievements were the first British atomic bomb (exploded in 1952) and hydrogen bomb (the plans for which were announced in 1955); the production of the most successful civil aircraft of the turbo-jet generation (the Viscount) and of the first aircraft to fly at over 1,000 m.p.h. (1956); and level competition with the USA (though it was not to be maintained) in the design and production of computers.

These were, too, the years in which 'automation' became a key-word, and also, more ominously, a bogey against which workers in fear of unemployment had to be constantly reassured. Not all progress was a matter of universal satisfaction, as that example shows. A case which was, and should not go unrecorded as a great technical achievement, was that in 1954 an Englishman was the first to run a mile in under four minutes.

The indications for the future were even more encouraging if the national mood were to rise to the occasion. The coming of the motorways was announced in 1955; so was the first programme of hospital-building since the war; so were plans for twelve nuclear power-stations. The same years saw the first introduction of legislation against restrictive practices and monopolies adversely affecting the public interest, which were the harbingers of later measures to restore genuine competition and protect the public against sharp practices. The first post-war expansion of universities and technical colleges also began at this time: more new universities were founded in the next decade than in any previous century of British history. Another visible sign of the times was a new style of building. Glass and concrete skyscrapers began to dominate the London skyline for the first time in the middle nineteen-fifties. Supermarkets similarly began to dominate the shopping centres. Both, of course, were imports from the USA; and they were accompanied—such is human nature—by a rising tide of anti-Americanism, especially after Suez.

There were many other less tangible contexts in which a turning-point can be located in or about the year 1956. What is common to all of them is a new, more modern style. The theatre felt the first impact of new playwrights treating the so-called 'Establishment' with anger and contempt. Whereas 1954 had been the year of nostalgic *pastiches* like *The Boy Friend* and *Salad Days*, 1955 was the year of anti-romantic realism in British drama, pioneered at Theatre Workshop in London's East End, followed by the era of the Royal Court Theatre from 1956 onwards. There was a similar mood of revolt—classless, anarchic, ferociously realist—in literature and the visual arts. A few outstanding names identify the new wave: John Osborne, Colin Wilson, Arnold Wesker, Kingsley Amis, John Bratby, Reg Butler; but many others could be cited. Perhaps the seminal work of the decade was Richard Hoggart's *The Uses of*

Literacy (1957), if only because the moving spirit of the cultural revival which was taking place, whether for good or ill, is aptly summarised in its sub-title: 'Aspects of working-class life with special reference to publications and entertainments'. But to speak of a cultural revival is not to suggest that the British public in general understood or liked the process of stirring up new life. There were also sharp reactions.

Public taste remained old-fashioned. It liked romance and royalty and tear-jerking sentiment, especially when they were combined, as at the death of King George VI (1952) or in the abortive romance of Princess Margaret (1955). It was not stirred by plays about homosexuals, which began to graduate from the theatre-clubs to the public stage about this time, or paintings of kitchen-sinks or sculptures of unknown political prisoners, or by *musique concrète*. It was stirred, on the contrary, by the last tram-journey in London, or the last steam loco-motive ever to be built, or the discovery of a temple of Mithras in the City of London, or the demolition of the Doric Arch outside Euston Station, or the interminable run of *The Mouse-trap*, all of which seemed to carry the folk-memory back to a vague remoteness of equal antiquity. If public taste was to be revitalised, it was not going to be done by the *avant-garde* in literature and the arts.

There were, however, more potent and immediate influences at work. One was the growth of foreign travel (and in particular of air travel) by people who before the war, and even before 1950, would seldom have taken their holidays further afield than Blackpool or Southend. Here was a direct result of in-creased prosperity and technological progress. Much more potent still was the arrival in September 1955 of Independent Television. It is perhaps this event more than any other which qualifies the middle years of the nineteen-fifties to be called a turning-point in the post-war history of Britain.

Clearly it is too early to assess the effect of commercial tele-vision on British society, but equally clearly it has been im-mense and permanent. At a few points the impact was marked without delay: the decline of the cinema (with a related up-surge of other amusements like bingo and bowling, which took over the vacant premises); a modification of style in BBC television induced by competition, which some called a deterioration; a demand for commercial radio, which was met initially by pirate-stations operating from ships or disused forts at sea outside territorial limits.

The impact on behaviour was more difficult to detect. Some blamed television in part for the increase in violence, hooliganism, crime, gambling, drunkenness, sexual immorality, drug-addiction and so on; but although these phenomena certainly increased simultaneously with the growing popularity of television, it could also be argued that these were separate products of a common sociological origin rather than cases of cause and effect. (It may also be noted that the same period saw a decline of religious conformity and church-going, despite the conscientious attention paid to them by all television programmes.) All that can confidently be said is that the arrival of commercial television was regarded with the utmost concern by the intellectuals of an older generation (of whom T. S. Eliot made himself the spokesman); and that ten years later Lord Hill, once the 'Radio Doctor' and now the Chairman of the Independent Television Authority, could say with perfect accuracy that even intellectuals watched commercial television regularly, though they did so, in contrast to the common man, with a sense of guilt.

No degree of qualification, in any case, can affect the conclusion that the arrival of independent television would by itself have made the middle years of the decade, which were precisely the years of Eden's premiership, a turning-point in our history. As it happens, this literally epoch-making event did not stand alone in marking the transition to the post-postwar world (the post-war world itself having been essentially continuous with the nineteen-thirties and forties).

Apart from the indicators that have already been mentioned, a few more may be added. People ceased to believe in the Cold War, especially after the Summit Meeting of 1955 and the visit to London of Bulganin and Khrushchev in 1956. Jealousy of the United States, and active delight in any setbacks suffered by the Americans, took its place. An attitude of resignation supervened towards the gradual dissolution of traditional links in the Commonwealth: the independence of Ghana in 1957 was a turning-point here, in a sense in which that of India had not been.

With the approaching independence of under-developed and non-selfsufficient states in the Commonwealth came an up-surge of conscience about overseas aid. Connected with the same movement of conscience were two other developments: a growing sense of the dangers of racial antagonism and a desire for the re-unification of the Christian Churches. None of the items in this catalogue of change was an event to which a date can be put. But the moment when each of them began to im-pinge unforgettably on the public's mind will be found in or around the years 1955–56. Before that period, they would have seemed just as foreign to post-war as to pre-war public opinion in Britain. There could be no clearer evidence of the essential continuity between the pre-war, war-time, and immediately post-war years.

Since these trends all had their source in earlier years, it would be absurd to seek a causal connection between them and the brief premiership of Anthony Eden, merely because it coin-cided with the moment when they broke the surface of our national stagnation. But it is not absurd to see a symbolic con-nection. These were the years of Eden in the sense that his was a peculiarly appropriate personality to preside over the end of an era which roughly coincided with his own political life.

It is also possible to see a catalytic connection between the calamity of Suez, which ended his career, and the abrupt con-frontation of the British people with the facts of life in the changed world they were living in. The essential nature of what had been happening to Britain was summarised in a notorious phrase used some six years later by Dean Acheson, the former US Secretary of State: 'Britain has lost an Empire and not yet found a role.' What was disquieting about the uproar caused in Britain by this simple statement of the obvious was that in 1962 it could still come as a surprise.

The lesson which was administered to the British people, though still imperfectly learned, at the end of 1956 can be briefly summed up. It was that super-states can do more or less what they like, subject to the restraints imposed by each other, because they enjoy the necessary power; sub-states (by which is meant the majority of the post-war influx into the United Nations) can also do so because they enjoy the necessary toleration; but the traditional nation-states cannot do so because they enjoy neither the power nor the toleration. The order of sovereignty to which Britain belongs was in the process of becoming obsolete. The question which faced the British people at the fall of Eden was: what was to be done about it? The end of 1956 marked not only a watershed but a parting of the ways. Two courses were open to us, and it looked as if the choice of the next Prime Minister would also be a choice between the two courses. The first was to defy the flowing tide of history and to make a final effort to assert complete national independence: this was the course which the French chose under de Gaulle two years later. The second was to accept the full logic of inter-dependence with its consequential sacrifice of national sovereignty; and this course could in practice only be pursued in union with Europe.

Few people in Britain saw the matter in those terms at the time. For most people the choice at the beginning of 1957 appeared to be between a man of decision and a man who could not make up his mind; a man who had been staunch and courageous both in the nineteen-thirties and in the crisis of 1956, and a man who had been weak and defeatist in both trials. The fact that Macmillan was pro-European and Butler much less so played no part in the choice. But the few who saw the matter in these terms must have thought that the choice of Macmillan to succeed Eden was in fact a choice of the second alternative. So it proved in the end, but only after another General Election in 1959. The first three years of Macmillan's long premiership were marked by a struggle to restore national independence; the last three by an acceptance of the need to achieve a new order of inter-dependent sovereignty. Both unfortunately proved equally abortive.

5

The False Dawn

THE SLOGAN of the Macmillan era was 'inter-dependence', but it was a word which meant different things at different times. Only from 1960 onwards was it accepted that inter-dependence included a substantial abrogation of national sovereignty. When that moment of acceptance came, it happened to coincide with a reversal of French policy, which had once been the main-spring of the European movement, but which now moved back in the direction of purely national sovereignty. Britain was thus out of step with France, for one reason or another, in both halves of the Macmillan era.

But what was even more serious, in the first three years of the post-Suez reconstruction, Britain was out of step with every-one else as well. The west Europeans, encouraged by the Americans, were advancing confidently towards economic and political unification, with a prospective enhancement both of their prosperity and of their status. To the British, however, inter-dependence still meant no more than practical arrange-ments of mutual co-operation. Organisations like NATO, OEEC and eventually EFTA were acceptable, because they did not involve any diminution of sovereignty. Supranational institutions like ECSC, Euratom and the Common Market were not, because they did.

Two crucial events marked the watershed of British history at the beginning of the new administration. In March 1957 the treaty creating the European Economic Community was signed in Rome by the six western powers, without Britain. In April a new British defence policy was announced ('the biggest change in military policy ever made in normal times', according to the White Paper). It was based on nuclear independence and a great reduction of conventional forces; but it paid lip-service to inter-dependence simply as a means of reducing costs by sharing overheads and technical experience. In the same month Macmillan met President Eisenhower in Bermuda, partly to rehabilitate the alliance after the breach over Suez, but also to recreate the old war-time arrangements for sharing defence secrets and responsibilities.

By the following year, it was agreed that the USA should share nuclear technology with Britain alone—a significant inroad upon the restrictions imposed by the McMahon Act of 1946, and one which exacerbated Anglo-French rivalry. But no British government had any substantial success in persuading the Americans to reciprocate defence orders by ordering British equipment and sharing the costs of our research and development.

American reluctance in this matter illustrated a deep-seated problem of the new technological era in Britain. To be competitive in the science-based industries, such as aircraft, aero-engines, nuclear energy, electronics, missile propulsion and so on, it is necessary to have both large capital resources and a large market. Even the American domestic market, utilising both military and civil production to share the vast overheads of research and development, is barely large enough. The overseas market is indispensable too, and this is secured by means of the well-planned distribution of dollar aid and loans. Britain single-handed cannot compete in any of these respects. Hence the need for inter-dependence in carrying the burden of technological development; but it cannot be inter-dependence solely with the USA, because then American industries would simply swallow up their British counterparts. Hence also the need for a large defence budget, because civil demand alone could not support the burden of overheads.

But at the same time the demands of the defence industries are in competition with civil industry for skilled man-power. Britain no longer possesses the scale of resources to compete with the USA in all these fields. The middle nineteen-fifties brought all these dilemmas to the surface. Ever since then, we have been trying (never successfully, and sometimes half-heartedly) to run as fast as we can in order to stay in the same place relative to the other powers.

It was impossible to contract out of the race, because in the last analysis the British people's standard of living depended on the balance of payments; and it was equally impossible to maintain a favourable balance on the basis of exports of the traditional secondary products which had made Britain's fortune in the past, such as cotton-cloth, or shipbuilding, or locomotives, because too many other countries had now reached the level of producing such manufactures themselves. Everything therefore depended on the advanced science-based industries in which competition with the USA was so formidable. But to emphasise the intrinsic difficulties is not to deny that bad mistakes were made. There was the abandonment of missile technology during several crucial years after the war. (Here the error was committed by the government's scientific advisers—a notable indication that the supposed infallibility of scientists in the twentieth century is very much a myth.) There was also the failure to exploit computers commercially: at the end of 1953 there were ten computers in operation in Britain compared with fifteen in the USA, but ten years later that narrow disparity had multiplied many times over. Above all, there was the miscalculation over economic and technical collaboration with Europe.

The aircraft and missile industries provide classic examples. All the technical and economic factors which pointed to the Anglo-French project of a joint supersonic passenger aircraft, the Concord, were calculable at least five years before the contract was signed. It could have been launched in 1957 instead of 1962, if the British government had not been committed to the policy of 'going it alone' which prevented us from accepting the Treaty of Rome. The same considerations apply to the missile Blue Streak, on which Britain's independent nuclear deterrent rested in the late nineteen-fifties, until strategic improvements in Soviet technology rendered it out of date and led to its cancellation in 1960. The rocket launcher was then merged in a joint civil project with several European powers and Australia, designed to put communications satellites into orbit—an ingenious salvage operation which might not have been necessary if the project had been planned from the first in a mood of international co-operation.

Complete national independence in a rapidly advancing technological age was simply beyond Britain's resources, but the possibilities of mitigating the burden by integration with Europe were not yet accepted.

Not only was the role of a great power in the outside world intolerable in itself: it was aggravated by lavish domestic policies associated with the welfare state. If the Conservatives had done what their enemies predicted on their return to office—cut the social services, accepted a level of unemployment around 3–4%, shifted the tax burden from direct to indirect taxation, and insisted on a general tightening of belts as in 1940—then it might have been possible both to carry the defence burden and to play an impressive, if never a dominant, role in foreign policy. But they did not do so. On the contrary, the cost of the welfare state was steadily expanded, wages and profits rose even faster, and indirect taxation was cut in almost every budget introduced by a Conservative Chancellor.

The long-term victim of this inflationary merry-go-round was naturally the balance of payments, especially in or immediately after the years of General Elections. In the thirteen years of Conservative administration from 1951, the years in which the balance of payments was in deficit were 1955 (an election year), 1960–61 (immediately following an election) and 1964 (another election year). The signs were plain that the public liked to be cajoled with easy money, and even in the year of the worst deficit (1964), they only put the Conservatives out of office by a very narrow margin.

Certainly the standard of living rose handsomely in those years. Critics were in the habit of stressing three qualifications, apart from the precarious balance of payments: that the rise was much smaller in real terms, owing to inflationary price-increases; that the neediest members of the community gained least, for the same reason; and that the increase of consumption was achieved at the expense of investment. All three qualifications contain some truth, but they need qualifying themselves.

It is true that wages and incomes consistently rose at a rate well in excess of the increase of production, and that measured by the Retail Prices Index the purchasing power of the pound consistently fell. But the same was happening in most industrial countries, including the USA, so that relatively Britain was not doing so badly as it seemed; and the rate of decline in the purchasing power of the pound was steadily reduced (from a rate of over one shilling in the pound *per annum* from 1945 to 1951 to a rate of well under sixpence in the pound *per annum* over the next twelve years).

It is also true that in the early post-war years, increases in pensions and insurance benefits fell below the rate of increase of prices; but in the nineteen-sixties, they did not. It is true, thirdly, that investment was often held back by deflationary measures such as the 'credit squeezes' of 1957 and 1961.

It is nevertheless also true that net capital investment at comparable prices more than doubled in the twenty years after the war. The very great increase in the national income also enabled increased public expenditure to be financed at lower rates of taxation.

Most striking of all is the evidence of individual savings, which multiplied about twenty times over the same period. People do not save unless they have confidence in their money, as well as a surplus over and above their daily needs. The simultaneous expansion on an enormous scale both of consumption and of savings might be thought to be clear evidence of a contented population. Up to 1959, when the Conservatives increased their electoral strength for the fourth consecutive time, there seemed to be no doubt that this was so. Yet in fact there was already a worm in the bud. Macmillan drew attention to it in July 1957 in a much misunderstood and misquoted speech, in which he said not only that 'most of our people have never had it so good,' but also that the problem of rising prices had not yet been brought under control. His point was to ask 'Is it too good to last?' He might also have asked 'Might it not be better still?'—provided that people were prepared to work a good deal harder in return for a rather slower increase of wages and incomes. Two shadows therefore fell over the prosperous years. One was a mood of uncomprehending discontent. The other was the perpetually frustrated search for an antidote to inflation, which eventually came to be labelled a 'prices and incomes policy'.

There was one sense in which the two shadows overlapped and darkened each other. The discontent and frustration were largely the product of the endless inflation of prices and also of the measures recommended to combat it. Experts agreed that a much slower rate of increase of wages was needed to keep prices within bounds. The first report of the Council on Prices, Productivity and Incomes (set up in July 1957) said as much, and urged the desirability of a 'perceptible margin of unemployment'. This theoretically impeccable advice was naturally unwelcome to Trade Unionists, who were bringing their standard of living up to that of the middle classes for the first time and did not intend to sacrifice it. There were the makings here of a direct conflict between government and unions, but the ultimate show-down was persistently avoided. Strikes multiplied —in ship-building, the docks, the railways, and for seven weeks in 1958—the last straw—on the London buses. But the result was self-defeating, especially in the last case, which brought discredit to its organiser, Frank Cousins, the General Secretary of the Transport and General Workers' Union, and helped to eliminate many redundant bus services for good. Militancy then reverted to words on both sides—the Trade Unions invariably passing resolutions denouncing wage restraint, and the Chancellor of the Exchequer warning all and sundry that arbitration could not be an unrestricted process but must be related to the public interest.

It was only when Chancellors operated directly on the economy by raising Bank Rate and enforcing deflation (as in September 1957 and July 1961) that any real effect was achieved; and that effect inevitably included unemployment and a retardation of investment as well as some improvement in the balance of payments. The improvement, moreover, such as it was, consisted of a reduction of imports rather than a substantial increase of exports, since exports could only expand if the domestic market was strong and active as well. New formulae had to be found; and all agreed, in theory at least, that they must include the modernisation of industry, the elimination of restrictive practices, and the expansion of competition. Yet in practice most attempts to achieve these aims were frustrated. There were notorious strikes over disputes between unions about the right to bore particular holes or make particular chalk-marks: the *ne plus ultra* was reserved for 1965, when strikes were caused by a foreman swearing at a worker and by a girl staying too long in the lavatory. These were only the most ludicrous symptoms of a general malaise.

The first attempts of the government to remove the last economic shackles of the war were too hesitant, and were bitterly resisted. A classic case was the Rent Act of 1957, which the Labour Party promised to repeal, though they only partially did so. Its real defect, economically speaking, was that it did not go far or fast enough in removing rent controls. Other efforts in the same direction were insufficiently bold and unconcerted: the introduction of the General Grant in place of specific Exchequer grants to local authorities (February 1957); the Royal Commission on the re-organisation of London's Government (July 1957); the measures to divert expanding industry from congested areas towards areas with more than 4% unemployment, which would once have been a very low figure (July 1958); the abolition of the Industrial Disputes Tribunal, on the ground that its decisions were unenforceable on the unions (October 1958); the plans to close 240 uneconomic collieries by 1965 and to reduce the miners' numbers by 11% (August 1959); and so on. The pace was too slow, the strategy was not apparent, and only grievances were created.

Not all the grievances were basically economic. Britain learned in the nineteen-fifties that prosperity too produces discontent, as well as crime-waves. The symptoms of discontent and the explosions of protest were too numerous to catalogue, but those which most impressed the government were probably three crucial by-elections: Gloucester (September 1957), Rochdale (February 1958) and Torrington (March 1958), all of which were disastrous for the Conservatives and encouraging for the Liberals even more than the Socialists. Voting Liberal was one popular way of protesting at this time, but there were many others. The heyday of the Campaign for

Nuclear Disarmament began in 1958, rather feebly matched by the League of Empire Loyalists on the extreme right. The new Homicide Act of 1957, the Wolfenden Report on sexual offences, the revision of the Betting and Gaming laws in 1959, the report of the Advisory Committee on the Treatment of Offenders opposing the re-introduction of corporal punishment—all these were occasions for the ventilation of extremist and eccentric opinions, passionately and militantly held. There were now not only 'angry young men' but angry middle-aged women.

Almost everyone could find something to be angry about. The maltreatment of Mau Mau prisoners at the Hola camp in Kenya; the arrest of Dr Banda for an imaginary conspiracy in Nyasaland (March 1959); a clout on the ear given by a policeman to a boy in Thurso, which led to a Tribunal of Enquiry and indirectly to a Royal Commission on the Police; the outbreak of racial disturbances in Nottingham and Notting Hill (August 1958); the publicity suddenly given to the Home Office's powers over telephone-tapping; the annoyance of the Press at being excluded from the meetings of certain local Councils, and the equal annoyance of the public at the intrusion of the Press into occasions of private grief—all these, and especially the uproar which they caused, were symptoms of a chronic malaise in which everyone seemed to have a grievance against someone else. It was natural to vent such feelings on the government. Yet by August 1958 the public opinion polls had already begun to swing back towards the Conservatives, and a year later they won their third consecutive General Election with a greatly increased majority.

Leaving aside all ancillary factors, the reason undoubtedly lay primarily in the shortcomings of the Labour Party, which was worse organised, worse financed, and far more divided than in 1955. The trouble had begun with the election of Gaitskell to succeed Attlee as party leader (December 1955). Attlee's leadership had been relatively non-controversial because he scrupulously avoided ever saying anything of the slightest interest. But Gaitskell expressed his views emphatically, and they lay so far to the right of his party that the *Economist* invented the term 'Butskellism' to describe the policies which he shared with Butler. Many doubted whether he was a Socialist at all, especially when he tried to revise Clause 4 (the nationalisation clause) of the party's charter in the aftermath of defeat in 1959.

His lack of grip on his colleagues was first acutely apparent at the Party Conference in 1958, when the leadership was attacked from the floor for its policies (or lack of them) over public schools, agriculture and nuclear weapons, among other subjects. It was also made painfully clear that the refusal of the Trade Unions to co-operate in a wages policy so long as a Conservative government was in office by no means implied that they would necessarily co-operate with a Labour government. The Labour Party defeated itself in 1959; yet Gaitskell was still widely regarded by the public as its greatest asset, whatever his colleagues might think.

It was characteristic of this period of uncomprehending frustration that those who were most vocal in protest were least representative of their fellows. Gaitskell's intellectual enemies in the Labour Party, ranging from the nuclear disarmers to Bevan and Wilson, cut no ice with the electorate or even with the rank and file of the party. This contrast was characteristic of the public mood at the time. It was matched in other contexts, which had little to do with politics. The arts and literature, for instance, were loud and active with highbrow protest. It was in 1959 that *Lolita* was published and in 1960 that *Lady Chatterley's Lover* was unsuccessfully prosecuted. The theatre of protest had expanded to include the theatre of the absurd, of horror, of cruelty, of anarchy; 'black comedy' was all the rage; the final triumph was achieved by a play in which a woman found expression by breaking wind at intermittent intervals, or another in which the characters disappeared slowly through the stage in successive acts.

Yet it is doubtful whether these symbols of protest against a decade of conservatism really chimed with the public mood. Every single year since the war broke records for the number of books published; but apart from a momentary flurry of excitement, it was not those destined to be accused by the police of obscenity which proved the best-sellers. Nor did the coach-loads of theatre-goers from the provinces converge on the theatre of cruelty: it was the Whitehall farces and, of course, *The Mousetrap* which drew them. Perhaps the most significant, because the most spontaneous, reaction of public opinion in these years was the outburst of fury over personal attacks on the Royal Family by Lord Altrincham and Malcolm Muggeridge (October 1957). Yet a notable improvement in the public relations of Buckingham Palace followed, and all were satisfied.

Nevertheless, the malaise was there, even if it failed to break effectively through the complacent surface until the middle sixties. It was latent in the very slogans current at the time. In 1959, the Conservatives won the General Election, whether they so intended or not, on the basis of such catch-phrases as 'I'm all right, Jack', and 'You've never had it so good'. At a sophisticated level of politics, the selfish materialism of such slogans offended the thoughtful minority which is, in the long run, the determinant of the style and quality of national life. But even at an unsophisticated level, they were self-defeating because they concealed their own contradictions. They could only be true for some people because they were untrue for others; and a competition in mere greed, such as they seemed to invite, was bound to be ruinous in the end.

Thus the harvest began to be reaped not very long after the Conservative triumph of 1959, first in economic troubles and later in symptoms of a moral decline. It was not simply that Tory freedom had failed to work. So far as the domestic economy was concerned it had worked exceedingly well. But it had failed to solve the major problem of fitting a reconstructed Britain into its international context. And in a wider sense, it had not merely worked but worked itself out.

6

Doubts Revived

THE SECOND half of the Macmillan era (1960–63) was in marked contrast with the first; and that not only because it ended in a melancholy failure. Macmillan was once accused of pointing to the right while he moved to the left. Possibly the same manœuvre was adopted by him in relation to Europe as well as to domestic policy; possibly he had made up his mind on the great revolution of policy which he launched in 1961, as long ago as 1958. It is at any rate important that he was the first British Prime Minister to undertake even one, let alone two, extensive tours of the Commonwealth (1958 and 1960) while in office; and he did so shortly before launching Britain on a new course which was bound to be bitterly criticised throughout the Commonwealth.

Certainly he foresaw the criticism: that was why the decision to apply for membership of the European Economic Community took so long to mature. Certainly, too, the criticisms were misconceived; for almost without exception, the Commonwealth countries stood to gain from Britain's participation in the EEC, which was in fact a belated response to a changing pattern of international trade, to which the rest of the Commonwealth had been reacting in anticipation for several years already. But it was probably from consideration of domestic problems primarily that the British decision was taken.

The Conservative government had restored prosperity and refrained from sabotaging the social revolution started by their predecessors. Indeed, in some minor respects they had even advanced it: it was the Conservatives who first breached the hereditary principle in the House of Lords, who strengthened the law to restrain monopolies and protect consumers, who first taxed capital gains, and who first devised a scheme for providing compensation to the victims of crimes of violence. But they had failed to achieve what the country really wanted, which was a return to greatness without any fundamental change in the British way of life.

The basic problem was psychological, as was often pointed out; but governments are in general unable to apply psychological remedies. Britain was like a man frustrated by his inability to get a quart out of a pint pot and yet determined not to part with his beloved pot. The government had spent years trying either to reconcile him to the size of the pot or to persuade him that he was in fact getting a quart out of it. Having failed to do either, Macmillan decided to buy him, willy-nilly, a larger pot, bearing the label 'Made in Europe'.

The economic motives underlying the decision to negotiate entry to the Common Market need either no elaboration or a vast deal of it. Here it is enough to say that it was seen firstly as a way of achieving a larger market and a larger source of capital, and secondly as a way of stimulating competition among both workers and managers. It was the one practicable cure for a situation in which Britain found herself to be the only political entity claiming to be a first-class industrial power on the basis of a population of less than a hundred millions—a situation which was already impossible to sustain. These motives were decisive in themselves, and no others are needed to justify the decision. But there were others, which were more intangible and arguable, and were therefore bitterly argued. They may be summed up in the proposition that the British people needed a revitalising shock. They had never recovered from the achievement of just, but only just, emerging victorious from the Second World War. To be overwhelmingly victorious, like the United States, was stimulating; to be crushed and over-run, like Germany, Japan, France and Italy, was an almost galvanic experience; but to be narrowly victorious, and to be convinced that the world owed us eternal gratitude, was demoralising.

Because it was not yet accepted that Britain had ceased to be a major power, there was deep suspicion of the government's motives in seeking entry into Europe, and suspicion was compounded by the refusal, or inability, of the government to parade the basic fact before the electorate, both because it would have been repudiated by the voters and because it would have weakened the country's bargaining position. Consequently the government had few friends during the early nineteen-sixties, except among the intellectual minority in the world of business and industry, journalism and the universities —and even among that minority there was probably not a majority that was temperamentally sympathetic to conservatism. It was no accident that the revival of the Labour Party's fortunes, and the final success of Gaitskell in recovering his grip on the party conference in 1961, came a few weeks after Macmillan announced to the House of Commons his intention to apply for admission to the Common Market. This dramatic event also coincided almost exactly with the 'credit squeeze' and the 'pay pause' imposed by Selwyn Lloyd as Chancellor of the Exchequer (July 1961). It was therefore an understandable suspicion that the government was not carrying out a carefully considered long-term policy but pursuing a counsel of despair, having lost control over events.

That this view was not confined to the Conservatives' congenital enemies was shown by the remarks of the Chairman of the Stock Exchange Council immediately before Selwyn Lloyd's second and last budget (March 1962): 'I believe that the City has very nearly reached the end of its tether, and that its loyalty and willingness to co-operate have almost reached breaking point.' In the same month the government suffered the crowning humiliation of losing the supposedly safe seat of Orpington to the Liberals at a spectacular by-election. The fact that the Liberals were in favour of entering the Common Market was irrelevant to the result. Indeed, they probably won many votes from anti-European Conservatives.

Although therefore Macmillan's motives for the great reorientation of British policy towards Europe were respectable, and indeed objectively ineluctable, it came at an unfortunate moment in the political climate. That this was equally true externally—as President de Gaulle showed by the humiliating rebuff of January 1963—should not obscure the fact that it was also true domestically. To that extent de Gaulle was right, not so much in challenging the bona fides of the British government's approach to Europe as in sensing that it had lost the confidence of the British people. There were a number of reasons why this loss of confidence came about in the early nineteen-sixties; and since it came so comparatively soon after the unprecedented electoral victory in 1959, it is evident that they were latent in the situation at an earlier date. The economic crisis and the European policy of 1961 only brought them to the surface.

Perhaps first place among the reasons should be taken by the feeling that Britain was no longer in command of her own destiny, let alone anybody else's. The feeling was of course corroborated by the decision to sign the Treaty of Rome, but it had already been stimulated, and continued to be stimulated, by great events in the world in which Britain appeared to play no part. President Eisenhower's visit to Britain in August 1959, and his appearance on television with Macmillan and other war-time leaders, seemed like a kind of epilogue to national greatness. After that—like the last Spitfire to take part in the RAF fly-past on 'Battle of Britain' day a few weeks later—the British people were as if relegated to the spectators' enclosure. What part had we in the 'space-race' between the USA and the Soviet Union, which reached level terms in 1960? The indirect answer was that we were still an advanced technological power, as witness the British lead in developing the Hovercraft and vertical take-off; but in the higher reaches, we had to abandon the task of developing single-handed such advanced projects as the Blue Streak rocket or the Blue Water missile; and we had to collaborate with the French in order to develop a supersonic passenger aircraft, the Concord. These were not symptoms of degeneration but merely indicators of comparative size and resources. International politics, however, respected only power.

The effort to recover power and status by pulling at our own boot-straps was already proving evidently too much for the British people. Modernisation was a favourite theme, but the implementation of it could only be a long-term process. There were, for instance, plans for establishing new Universities and

Colleges of Advanced Technology on a spectacular scale: five new ones were announced in 1960. But their undoubted value undoubtedly lay in the future; and meanwhile there was the so-called 'brain-drain' of scientists and technicians to the USA—a movement which would once have been regarded as a symptom of imperial destiny, but was now a symptom of decline. There was a massive effort to modernise the transport system, with a special concern for the railways, which were costing the tax-payer well over £100 million a year; but the appointment of Dr Beeching as Chairman of British Railways (November 1962) could not bear fruit in under five years, by which time another government had forced his resignation. There was also a valiant attempt by Selwyn Lloyd, usually condemned as an unimaginative Chancellor of the Exchequer, to modernise and plan the economy by setting up the National Economic Development Council and (less successfully) the National Incomes Commission; as well as by introducing the so-called 'regulators' to enable indirect taxation to be varied at any time of year instead of only in the Budget. But not only was the value of these internal innovations not immediate; they were also largely frustrated by another major economic crisis in the middle of 1961.

Hence Britain had little part in the great world events of 1960–62. The disaster of the American U2 aircraft, shot down over Russia as the abortive Summit Conference was about to open in Paris in May 1960; the public eruption of the Sino-Soviet dispute in the same year; the catastrophe in the Congo and the revolt in Angola during 1960–61; the confrontation of Khrushchev and President Kennedy in Vienna (June 1961); the Berlin crisis culminating in the erection of the Wall between east and west (August 1961); the renewal of nuclear tests by the Soviet Union and then by the USA (September 1961); the beginnings of the break-up of the Central African Federation, so hopefully put together by Britain in 1953; the Chinese attack on India (October 1962); and finally the apocalyptic climax over Cuba, a few weeks later in 1962: in all these events the role of Britain, though not always negligible, was never in the front rank.

There was a deep and widespread anxiety at the thought that the British people were now rather the victims of events than the masters of them—a feeling which had been part of the inheritance of other peoples for generations, but was entirely new in Britain. It was observed, too, that all these dramas involved one or other of two themes: Africa (which meant problems of race) and nuclear weapons. Racial problems and nuclear warfare now began to pre-occupy public opinion to an overwhelming degree. The assumption was that a government which could not control them was not master in its own house.

The problem of race has both its domestic and its external aspects, which Macmillan brought together in his celebrated speech on 'the wind of change' in Cape Town in February 1960. It was a statement both of Britain's philosophy of race relations, as contrasted with apartheid, and also of the concept of African independence. But it was also seen, not without justice, as a largely theoretical commentary on a situation over which Britain had ceased to have any control. The racial riots in England, the imminent disruption of the Central African Federation, the murder of Lumumba in the Congo (February 1961), the emergence of the rival groupings of African nationalists, the Civil Rights movement in the USA, were all symptoms of a tragic trend which no talk of a 'wind of change' by a British Prime Minister could mitigate or alter. It was even argued that the only direct effects of Macmillan's speech were the massacre of Africans at Sharpeville a few weeks after it and the secession of South Africa from the Commonwealth in 1961. Even the disastrous crisis over Rhodesia's unilateral declaration of independence in 1965 could be attributed by bitter white Africans to the things that Macmillan said and did five years earlier.

Opinion in Britain was sharply divided on these matters. Though few doubted the inevitability of African independence, which even took on a slightly improved aspect when Nigeria became independent in October 1960, in circumstances diametrically contrasting with the chaos in the Congo, there was equally little confidence that Africans would make a success of running their own affairs; and this judgement was confirmed

66

by revolution even in Nigeria a few years later (January 1966). Judgements on South Africa and Rhodesia were also affected by the anxieties arising from the growing influx of coloured immigrants into Britain, though paradoxically it was the arrival of seemingly inexhaustible floods of Indians and Pakistanis, most of whom could speak no English, that influenced emotional opinion much more than that of the relatively Anglicised West Africans and West Indians. Until 1960 the government clung to the principle of free entry from the Commonwealth into the United Kingdom. But there was strong pressure for restrictions, which was not confined to the Conservative right wing. It was just as strong, though better camouflaged, from the Trade Unions as from the neo-fascist groups, which had re-emerged in this unhappy period under leaders like Colin Jordan.

At last, when the influx rose to a rate of about 120,000 *per annum* in 1961, the government introduced restrictive legislation with great reluctance. The Labour Party in opposition voted against the Commonwealth Immigrants Bill at every stage, but prudently refrained from promising to repeal it. On July 1, 1962, the day it became law, the neo-fascists held a public meeting in Trafalgar Square which the Communists violently broke up—a phenomenon scarcely experienced in Britain since before the war. It looked as if the government had acted only just in time, and perhaps too late to save their credit. They were blamed both by those with a strongly racialist outlook (for not going far enough) and by those who sympathised with the coloured immigrants, and of course by the ex-colonial governments and potential immigrants themselves. The painful problem undoubtedly had some effect on voting patterns at the General Election in 1964, though probably on balance the Labour Party lost as many votes as it won on the racial issue, especially since it reversed its attitude shortly before the election. What matters most to the contemporary historian was that it had become a seemingly insoluble problem over which no British government could exercise complete control.

The other shadow hanging over Britain in the early nineteen-sixties, which the government seemed powerless to disperse, was that of the nuclear deterrent, as the hydrogen-bomb was euphemistically called. There were rational reasons for arguing, as Churchill had argued as long ago as 1954, that the world was safer under this shadow than it had ever been before, whether or not Britain possessed a nuclear weapon of her own. Certainly there had been, in the twenty post-war years, at least a dozen international crises of at least Balkan magnitude, and of a kind which half a century earlier would infallibly have led to a local war and very probably to a general war as a consequence; but today none had done so.

It was difficult to dispute that the reason lay partly in the mutual fear induced in the great powers by the existence of the nuclear threat (as exemplified by the Cuba crisis of 1962) and partly in the consequential determination and the enhanced capacity of the great powers to isolate, limit and contain local wars between lesser powers (as exemplified by the clash between India and Pakistan in 1965). War had in fact become both prohibitively expensive to pursue and much easier to stop.

But reactions to the nuclear threat were not purely rational. What became known as 'living in the shadow of the bomb' induced in a significant and vocal minority an irrational and almost neurotic emotion. How irrational and neurotic it was can be seen by observing that the only way in which the so-called 'unilateralists' could have been proved right in their forebodings would have been if someone had deliberately dropped the bomb; so that they were in the position of simultaneously wishing to be right and dreading the only way of proving it. Their seeming schizophrenia thus had at least a basis in logic.

The wave of emotion on the subject reached its high tide in the years 1960–62. Thereafter the concentration on a single theme was dissipated in half a dozen miscellaneous causes such as apartheid in South Africa or political prisoners in Greece. It was in January 1960 that demonstrators at American aerodromes in Britain became the first crusaders since the militant suffragettes to court imprisonment deliberately for a political cause. Passions grew stronger as the nuclear programme unfolded, with its clear theme of inter-dependence with the USA.

The crucial stages were the decision to establish an early warning station at Fylingdales (February 1960) and to base American Polaris submarines in Holy Loch (November 1960); the destruction over Russia of an American RB.47 aircraft based in Britain, even though it carried no weapons (July 1960); the decision to abandon Blue Streak and replace it with the American air-borne Skybolt missile (March 1960), itself later to be replaced by the sea-borne Polaris a few years later; and the general renewal of nuclear tests after a moratorium since 1958, for which left-wing opinion in Britain blamed the USA more severely than the Soviet Union, despite (or perhaps because of) the fact that the Russians did it first. In these years the Easter march of the Campaign for Nuclear Disarmament from Aldermaston to London became almost a mass popular demonstration; and one Trade Union after another passed 'unilateralist' resolutions, until Gaitskell and his supporters regained control in 1962.

An important and novel aspect of the public mood during this period was the activity in support of it of very young people. Since the middle nineteen-fifties, which have already been marked as a turning-point, a new generation had reached maturity which barely, if at all, remembered the war, and to whom the agonies and passions of the nineteen-thirties were ancient history. Both unemployment and conscription had been abolished. In every material respect the young were much to be envied in comparison with their counterparts before the war, or even in the first post-war decade. They were better fed and stronger; they had better chances of staying on at school, getting a safe job or going on to a university, and of turning up to work on a moped or even in a motor car. The annual report of the Chief Medical Officer at the Ministry of Health in 1959 said that children of twelve were two to four inches taller than fifty years earlier, but 'prone to obesity due to sweets'.

The ominous hint that discipline was the main thing they lacked persisted, and grew stronger as they grew older. Juvenile crime and hooliganism (especially at seaside resorts during bank holidays) became a major scandal. Religion declined, sexual precocity and drug addiction advanced among teenagers.

Crime became not only lucrative but glamorous: the theft of the Goya portrait of the Duke of Wellington from the National Gallery (August 1961) and the Great Train Robbery (August 1963) appealed to a morbid streak in the public imagination. It was hardly surprising that young people came to look on moral and legal inhibitions with contempt. It became fashionable on the one side to denounce young people generally as uncontrollably immoral, and on the other to justify or at least account for their conduct in terms of 'living under the shadow of the bomb'.

Both these arguments were nonsensical. Both ignored the fact that only an exhibitionist minority was involved. Much more impressive, though less publicised, were the enthusiasm of the young for good causes, both at home and abroad; their alertness and activity and lack of inhibition; their desire to be creative and effective, not simply spectators of events. These instincts could of course be channelled into bad courses as well as good; but except when they were so channelled, they usually found good causes if left to themselves. The young of the early nineteen-sixties questioned everything and took nothing for granted; they found a free-masonry of youth across international boundaries. They developed an unprecedented taste for the arts in unforeseen ways: for music, both popular (like the Proms) and more popular still (like the beat groups); for the off-beat drama, which became almost the staple fare of television; above all for satire, which grew into a major industry.

Their political sense may have been immature, but at least they had one, which is more than could have been said for the pre-war generation. It would have been far less absurd to give votes at eighteen in the nineteen-sixties than in the nineteen-thirties. The odd thing is that the clamour for this particular reform became loud only when conscription and capital punishment (both of which began to be applicable at eighteen) were in the process of abolition.

As usual in dealing with human beings, to generalise is to falsify. But it is an unquestionable generalisation that those who reached voting age for the first time in the nineteen-sixties could barely remember what it was like to live under

70

any but a Conservative government. Believing, as is eternally necessary to human happiness, that what seemed wrong could be remedied, and also (with less foundation in fact) that everything was the fault of the government, young voters had a natural inclination by 1964 to vote Liberal or Labour. Their elders, though also once more disillusioned, were more cautious: hence the narrowness of the result when the General Election came. The point was that there were only two alternative governments, and neither had given the British people the whole of what it wanted in the twenty years since the war. It was arguable, therefore, though far from generally accepted, that what they really wanted was in its totality unattainable; that the trouble with Britain was not political or administrative or personal, but structural. This was of course Macmillan's thesis, and his reason for seeking a re-construction in the larger international context of Europe. But quite apart from the French rebuff in January 1963, he had not succeeded in convincing the British people of his thesis.

Public opinion comprises a wide range of individual opinions, and no eclectic summary of views on Europe can be universally valid. The more far-seeing of the younger voters, particularly in the newer types of professions, were probably persuaded on the whole by Macmillan's logic; the older generation were more impressed by the reasoning of the Beaverbrook Press. But there were innumerable cross-currents of opinion at every level in 1963–64. It was perhaps not so much the attempt to enter Europe which helped to lose the 1964 election as the failure to succeed in that attempt. It was also many other things, some already mentioned, such as the feeling that Britain had undeservedly fallen back in the international order; and some that were trivial or irrelevant. Anyone who has ever canvassed a parliamentary constituency can confirm that the reasons for voting or not voting are unpredictable and sometimes breathtaking. But some of the influences at work towards the end of the Macmillan era are clearly identifiable, even if few voters would consciously and explicitly have identified them.

The Conservative government had failed to manage the

economy with consistent effectiveness. When the economy went up, admittedly it always went up higher and higher; but it never ceased also intermittently to go down. (The mistake was to lead people to believe that it could ever be otherwise.) The Conservatives incurred widespread antagonism—not only among the immediate victims—by firmly enforcing the 'pay pause' against the only people on whom they actually could enforce it: their own employees, the nurses, teachers and post-men. They had only partially solved the many intricacies of the housing problem: rents had been dealt with in part, rating hardly at all. (The mistake was not to have tackled these problems much more ruthlessly and rapidly at the first moment of coming into office, since they needed at least ten years to work themselves out.) They had failed to see in time the evils of the uncontrolled speculator in land and property of whom Rachman was the most notorious example. (The mistake could have been avoided by earlier abolition of rent restriction, which alone made Rachmanism possible, coupled with a heavier rate of tax on capital gains than that half-heartedly imposed in the Budget of 1962.) They had failed to control the activities of irresponsible elements in the Trade Unions: so, of course, had the leaders of the TUC, despite many protestations of good intentions. Above all they had been guilty of two related failures. They had given an impression of moral deterioration in public life, and they had acquired a hostile Press.

There was a large element of bad luck about these two dis-advantages. The impression of moral decay was primarily associated with the name of Profumo and the gallery of notorious figures associated with him. But it must be added that Britain was also earning a reputation as an international centre of strip-tease, prostitution and obscene literature, which the British people have always preferred to associate with Paris. The damage done by the Profumo affair was made enormously worse by the vindictiveness of the Press, stimulated by resentment of the imprisonment of two journalists for refusing to disclose sources of information to the tribunal of enquiry into the case of the Admiralty spy, Vassall (March 1963). The connection between all these sordid matters lay in the fact that

Macmillan had been reluctant to dismiss Profumo in good time because he had made an earlier error of judgement in unnecessarily accepting the resignation of an innocent junior minister implicated by the imprisoned journalists in the Vassall case.

The best that can be said of the whole melancholy episode is that Macmillan was clearly losing his grip on events. This judgement only confirmed the impression of a year earlier, when Macmillan dismissed seven of his Cabinet (including the Chancellor of the Exchequer, Selwyn Lloyd) on a single day in July 1962. Even his success in contributing to the establishment of a partial nuclear test-ban treaty with the USA and the Soviet Union (August 1963) was of small avail, since most of his critics regarded the British contribution to it as negligible. The illness which forced his resignation in October 1963 was in a sense a merciful release, but it was far from being the end of the Conservatives' troubles. It was rather the beginning of a prolonged crisis in their party leadership.

Although the only valid criticism of the succession of Home to Macmillan as Prime Minister lay against the method of carrying it out, there was a widespread feeling that the Conservatives had taken a reactionary step back into an archaic system. In fact the government's efforts to restore its standing by a drastic campaign of modernisation were, if anything, intensified after the change of leadership. The reflation of the economy in the wake of the 'pay pause' continued unabated, with massive programmes of public expenditure projected over the next five years. The programme was based on the calculation of the National Economic Development Council (created by Selwyn Lloyd not long before his dismissal) that production could expand at the rate of 4% per annum, coupled with a rate of increase of wages not exceeding 3%; but both figures were severely criticised by the Labour opposition, who did nothing to discourage the Trade Unions from helping to make both unattainable. The programme included a huge expansion of the already considerable programme of building roads, houses, hospitals, schools and universities, the strain of which was likely to fall on the construction industries even more severely than on the budget. It also provided for raising the school-leaving age to sixteen by 1970, which was a logical step since the war-time 'population bulge' would by then have passed through their secondary education and the next wave of population-expansion would not yet have arrived.

Home's government re-affirmed all these projects. During its short life (1963–64), it went even further. The Robbins and Newsom Reports on university and secondary education were accepted instantly with little consideration of their implications. Legislation was introduced to restrict the practice of 're-sale price maintenance' in the last year of the parliament, with respectful regard for the powerful logic of Heath at the Board of Trade but little for the prejudices of Conservative supporters in marginal constituencies. The troubled progress of this Bill through Parliament suggested that the re-formed government had still not recovered its grip. So did the comment of the Prime Minister that the economy had never been stronger, in February 1964, the day before the trade figures revealed an adverse balance of £120 million in a single month. So did the *Memoirs* of Lord Kilmuir, the Lord Chancellor whom Macmillan had dismissed two years earlier, when they were published in April 1964. So did the unsavoury episode of a profit of £4 million made by Ferranti's on a government contract, unknown to the Ministry of Aviation. The Conservative administration was as unmistakably moving to its demise as its predecessor in 1905, and for not dissimilar reasons.

Yet the outcome was very unlike 1905. The Labour Party won the General Election of 1964 not by a landslide but by the narrowest margin of the century; and the Liberals, though they won only nine seats (plus a tenth at an early by-election) came nearer to holding the balance of power than at any time since 1924. The vote of no-confidence in the Conservatives was clear, the vote of confidence in the Socialists much less so. If this had been a conscious, articulate verdict on the part of the British people, it might have been a just one. It could have been interpreted as meaning that the British people had passed through the last illusion. They had seen at last, it could have been argued, that Britain's problems were structural and deep-seated; that the Conservatives had belatedly appreciated the fact, but proved unable to carry through the necessary reconstruction; that the Socialists had failed to appreciate it (or anyway, to admit it), but that they might prove more competent to deal with the structural problems once forced by experience of office to confront them. Unfortunately, this was probably not the meaning of the verdict.

The Conservatives lost office not only for their defects but for their merits; not only for the 'pay pause' and the Profumo scandal, but also for trying to enter Europe and abolishing resale price maintenance. The Socialists barely scraped home on the benefit of the doubt. They lost votes from the assumption that they intended to nationalise steel, abolish capital punishment, renew unrestricted immigration, and abandon Britain's nuclear weapons. They gained votes both from those who wanted these things and from those who assumed (rightly, as it turned out) that they would default on most of them. The outcome was therefore determined by a mutual cancellation of factors which left an equation reading little more than 'six of one equals half a dozen of the other'. Thus did the British people in 1964 get the government they deserved.

7

The End of Illusions

THE GENERAL ELECTION of 1964 was only the second since the war that changed the party in power. The pattern of events was curiously similar to that of 1951 in reverse. Both elections were exceedingly close; on both occasions the new government soon had to deal with a frightening economic crisis, though opinions naturally differed about the causes of the crisis in each case. Both incoming governments inherited a state of undeclared war in the Far East and of imminent revolt in Central Africa. As in 1951, so in 1964, the new government carried an excessive load of election promises, and was soon accused of broken pledges. On both occasions the General Election was followed next year by an exceedingly complex Finance Bill which required an unprecedented number of amendments at the Committee stage. On both occasions, too, the defeated party was soon embroiled in internal disagreements and criticism of its leadership.

The repetition of the pattern on each occasion was ominous. It inevitably left cynics with the impression that 'this is where we came in', and that the same cycle of history was about to recur. There was in fact, as there had been again and again since 1945, a basic continuity with relatively minor changes. But what Britain needed was, on the contrary, discontinuity and radical change.

The Labour Party had certainly promised change. Words like 'dynamic' and 'progressive' were constantly on the lips of Wilson and his colleagues. He established several new Ministries, of which the most important were the Department of Economic Affairs (to take over from the Treasury the function of activating the economy as distinct from controlling the budget) and the Ministry of Technology. Among his much enlarged list of Ministers and advisers he included several appointments from outside Westminster and Whitehall, which were symbolic rather than effectual: Cousins from the Transport and General Workers' Union, Lord Snow and Lord Bowden, Kaldor and Balogh from the academic world; and *The Times'* defence correspondent, who had hitherto declared himself a Liberal.

But the most noticeable things about the new administration were those that had not changed, despite expectations raised before the election. These included a wide range of policies such as relaxing immigration controls, abandoning Britain's nuclear deterrent, nationalising the steel industry, appointing an Ombudsman, repealing the Rent Act of 1957—not all of which were promised so explicitly during the election as they had seemed to be a year or two earlier. In almost every case mentioned, the reversal of policy by the Labour Party was to be welcomed on grounds of national interest. But in all such cases there was an overwhelming impression left that a change of government meant little change of policy at all.

Labour supporters were naturally more disappointed than Conservatives that this proved to be so. Their disappointment was bitterest over two particular sectors of policy: finance and defence. The crisis of sterling in the month following the Socialists' accession to power was met by impeccably orthodox measures which they had denounced in opposition as 'stop-go'. The problems of defence were confronted with a slight recasting of Britain's chosen role, whose centre of gravity was to lie in future 'east of Suez', and the cost was somewhat reduced by cancelling a number of advanced weapons-systems, such as the TSR.2. But the defence budget still remained around £2,000 million a year; the British nuclear weapons were not scrapped; and the policy of supporting the Americans in South-East Asia became, if anything, more unconditional than before. The effect of all these unexpected developments on public opinion was remarkable. The Labour Party lost support on its left wing, which argued that if the country was to be governed on Conservative principles in any case, it might just as well be under a government which openly professed them.

77

But it gained support among the marginal voters, who had been reluctant to support it in 1964 from the very fear that it might do exactly what it said it would do.

From another and perhaps more serious point of view, the credit and the discredit were equally irrelevant. What mattered was that the themes of the Labour Party's programme before and even immediately after the General Election implied that there was nothing wrong with Britain which could not be cured by adjustment and stimulation; that the defects were not structural but personal and administrative. These were themes of precisely the kind that the public wanted to hear. Voters were all the more justified in giving the Labour Party another chance because they heard almost no countervailing theme. The rebuff to the British government by de Gaulle in 1963 had rendered entry into Europe almost nugatory as an election issue; and de Gaulle himself appeared to be bent on wrecking what remained of the EEC. Yet in fact the structural problem remained intact. It remained just as true as at any time in the preceding decade that a country with the population and material resources of the traditional nineteenth-century nation-state could not keep up with twentieth-century super-states on its own. The fact that de Gaulle was engaged in a massive confidence trick to prove the contrary on behalf of France could not alter reality in the long run. The Labour Party gave many indications in 1964 that it shared something of the French delusion.

The most notable example was its attitude to relations with Europe and the Commonwealth. Gaitskell had taken a passionately hostile attitude towards the negotiations with the EEC in the months before his death, with a memorable catch-phrase about 'turning our backs on a thousand years of history'. The phrase caught the mood of the Labour Party, though one or two leading figures (notably George Brown and Roy Jenkins) tried to redress the balance. In sober reality, we were much nearer to having a thousand years of history in common with Europe than with most of the Commonwealth. But it was towards the Commonwealth that the Labour Party decided to turn when it conceded rather half-heartedly that 'splendid isolation' was impossible. There could be no question, naturally, of an integration of economies with the Commonwealth, consisting as it did of countries at every imaginable stage of development and of every imaginable size, as there could have been with the European Six. That indeed was what appealed to the Labour Party and to many Englishmen about the Commonwealth: commitments could always be limited, varied and flexible. Wilson's early foreign policy was therefore directed to conciliating the Commonwealth, especially the newer members, at the expense of Europe.

Many gambits were tried, both direct and indirect. Friendliness towards Commonwealth immigrants was indicated by an ill-judged attack in the Prime Minister's first speech on the Address, directed against a new Conservative MP who had defeated Labour's shadow Foreign Secretary, Gordon Walker, in a campaign alleged to have been based on racialism. The designation of Gordon Walker, a former Secretary of State for Commonwealth Relations, as Foreign Secretary (though he had to resign after twice failing to be elected to parliament) was itself another indication of the trend of Wilson's thinking. So was the character of the import surcharge imposed in October 1964 to relieve the balance of payments, which severely affected all European countries (especially our fellow-members of the European Free Trade Association) but much less severely the under-developed Commonwealth countries, since all raw materials—their main exports—were exempt.

Perhaps the most marked indication of the new policy, however, was the strong hint given in the first Economic White Paper that the Anglo-French supersonic passenger-aircraft project, the Concord, was to be cancelled. By labelling it a 'prestige project', the government showed simultaneously its contempt for the French as well as for the previous government, and also its failure to understand the character of modern technology and the structural nature of Britain's problems. By changing its mind at the end of the year, the government also showed its ability to learn quickly and to reverse its errors of judgement.

The Concord, whether it would ultimately succeed or not,

was a symbol and a portent of the most crucial significance. Many lessons about contemporary Britain can be drawn from it. One is that Britain cannot carry the burden of modern advanced technology single-handed, because the market for such developments is too small to admit international competition between more than two or three powers, of whom the USA and the Soviet Union are bound to be two. The inference from these two lessons is that partnership is inevitable, and it can only work satisfactorily with a power of equal industrial capacity (such as France), not with one of much greater capacity (such as the USA) or much less (such as the rest of the Commonwealth). A third lesson is that if the British aircraft industry is to survive, it must have a closely integrated programme of civil and military development combined, in order to spread the overheads economically; and a fourth is that there is no absolute dividing line between the aircraft and other industries, particularly electronics—hence the neologism of 'avionics'. The inference from these two lessons is that the British industries concerned are bound to be heavily dependent on government orders, and must necessarily concentrate into fewer and larger units. The Conservative government tried to apply these lessons, against strong resistance, in 1960. They were re-emphasised by an enquiry into the aircraft industry under Lord Plowden in 1965.

The inferences were somewhat slowly absorbed by the Labour government. Perhaps the most attractive to them was that there was a good non-dogmatic case for nationalising the aircraft industry; but although there would be no particular harm in this step, there would be little good either, since it would leave the structural problem unsolved. Considerations of the same kind applied to the nuclear industry, which was of course already nationalised, though at the same time it drew substantially upon private enterprise in engineering technology. It was impossible for Britain to be a nuclear power in complete isolation, whether in the military or the civil sense (since the two were likewise inseparable). That was true for technical and economic reasons as well as political. In this field, too, partnership was necessary, but it was much less obvious with whom.

The Commonwealth was clearly ruled out. The USA was co-operative to a certain extent, but with the usual reservations and limitations. Europe was again theoretically the right direction in which to look. But partnership with France was restricted by the extreme nationalism of de Gaulle in nuclear matters, and with Germany by both historic suspicion and formal treaties.

For some months Wilson tried to reconcile these intractable factors with his own pledge to 'abandon the pretence of an independent nuclear deterrent' by means of a complex device to be known as the Allied Nuclear Force. The plan was a variant of, and a substitute for, an earlier American plan known as the Multilateral Force, which was regarded with extreme suspicion by the Labour Party, for fear that it would give too much power over nuclear policy to the German Federal Republic. It is hardly necessary to examine these two intricate devices in detail because, in the words of a witty Labour back-bencher, the only function of the ANF was to sink the MLF, which it successfully did. The government was thus left at the end of the process with a defence policy which differed only marginally from that of its predecessor. The two substantial differences were a shift of emphasis in the direction of 'East of Suez' and an attempt to economise by cancelling all new aircraft-carriers and several advanced aircraft projects (including the TSR.2, although it had already flown) and virtually abolishing the Territorial Army. No attempt had been made to resolve the structural problem, which was, in this context, that Britain could not remain a major military power occupying bases all over the world entirely at her own expense; still less could she combine such a role with the maintenance of a nuclear force.

Once the realities of the situation began to become plain, it was reasonable to suppose that the government would recognise that they dictated a renewed effort to enter a comprehensive partnership with Europe, since neither the Commonwealth nor the USA (though for opposite reasons) could make an acceptable partner. As the warning symptoms accumulated during the government's first year of office, there were some signs that the lesson had been learned, at least by the new

81

Foreign Secretary, Michael Stewart, and other members of the Labour Party's right wing.

The symptoms were indeed unmistakable. Britain's comparative impotence in the world of super-states was emphasised by events abroad over which the British people not only had no control but no power even of significant reaction: for instance, the first Chinese nuclear explosion and the fall of Khrushchev, both on the very day Labour came to power; the deteriorating state of war in Vietnam, where Wilson's attempts to intervene by means of a Commonwealth mission or the dispatch of past and present Ministers met only humiliating rebuffs; the striking advances of the USA and Soviet Union in space technology, where Britain was overtaken even by France with her own national programme.

Even in the Commonwealth Britain found herself challenged and often helpless: for example over the disruption of the Federation of Malaysia and the breakdown of the negotiations for a federation of Aden and the South Arabian sheikhdoms (both in August 1965), the brief war between India and Pakistan (September 1965), the unilateral declaration of independence by Rhodesia (November 1965) and the revolutions in Nigeria and Ghana (January and March 1966). Our status as bystanders was emphasised in both foreign and Commonwealth affairs when the heads of the Indian and Pakistan governments accepted an invitation from the Soviet Prime Minister to meet and compose their differences in Tashkent. It was the first time that so important an intra-Commonwealth occasion had taken place under non-British auspices. In the same month (January 1966) there took place an equally significant event at Lagos in Nigeria: the first conference of Commonwealth Prime Ministers ever to be held outside London, and one at which the British Prime Minister was in a sense put in the dock for the British government's handling of the crisis in Rhodesia.

Britain had indeed 'lost an Empire and not yet found a role', in Acheson's words. There were few consolations in the outside world, and the list shows how meagre they were: the success of the Queen's state visit to Germany (May 1965); the warm welcome accorded to Wilson and other Ministers on their visits to Washington; progress towards the restoration of constitutional government and independence in British Guiana; the general impression that the Prime Minister had enhanced his stature by his handling of the Rhodesian crisis. Some perverse satisfaction was even felt in Britain at the sight of de Gaulle doing his utmost to disrupt the Common Market, as though it showed how wise or lucky we had been to have no part in it. No such satisfaction was publicly expressed by Ministers, of course, but it was felt by the public, and nothing was said or done to discourage it.

It was a short-sighted policy of silence and detachment, since the relative retrogression of the European movement of unification between 1963 and 1966 in fact offered Britain a valuable opportunity of moving back towards engagement in Europe. But to take the opportunity would have involved recognising the structural character of our problems and making some fundamental adjustments to meet them; and of this there was no sign up to the end of 1965. The signs of a change of heart in 1966 could not alter the fact that another two years had been lost. Two examples may be quoted of radical steps which would have indicated such a recognition if taken in time, but which were not taken. They concern firstly the aircraft industry, to which some reference has been made above, and secondly agriculture.

The conclusion that the British aircraft industry was too large in man-power, relative to its market, and too small to compete over the whole range of research, development and production with the USA, was correctly argued by the first Socialist Minister of Aviation, Roy Jenkins, who was incidentally one of the few pro-Europeans in his party. He stated it in connection with the cancellation of the TSR.2 and other advanced military aircraft. But instead of then pursuing more whole-heartedly the policy of integration with the European aircraft industries, which had been inaugurated with the Concord and other projects inherited by the new government, the decision was taken to fill the gaps created by cancellations with American aircraft. The reasons for doing so were cogent: it was a question of fulfilling the services' requirements with the most suitable aircraft available in time. But it was a grave blow to the British aircraft industry as the spearhead of British technology. For whereas the British industry could collaborate with the French and German industries on equal or superior terms, it could only function as a satellite in relation to the American industry. These were decisions which could never be reversed, in the sense that the lost ground could not be regained.

They were dictated by the familiar argument that the services must always have the best that is available. Such perfectionism was difficult to rebut in debates which easily became emotional, but in fact it was a case of the best being the enemy of the good. The logical conclusion of the argument was either that the services would get no aircraft at all because there was no limit to the possibility of improvement up to and beyond the moment of flight, or that they would be delivered too late. Much the same considerations applied to civil aircraft, which had to be minutely tailored to the requirements of the national Corporations. The RAF, the Navy, BOAC and BEA all had overlapping requirements, but they seldom shared an aircraft because each had to have its own ideal realised. The results were exorbitant costs, late deliveries, lost export orders, and a declining industry. It could have survived and prospered as part of an integrated European industry; but the urgent and bold decisions necessary to that end were not taken.

The second example, that of agriculture, shows the antipathy of the Labour government towards a European solution with even greater clarity, because the decisions were taken consciously and deliberately. If Britain were ever to become economically a part of Europe, it would be necessary to alter the basis of support for agriculture from the British to the continental system: the converse was obviously impossible to expect. The continental system relied on external tariffs to maintain reasonable prices for their own farmers' products; the British system on subsidies to the farmers and free entry for overseas products (an invaluable boon to the Commonwealth) to keep prices down for the consumer. The essential difference was that under the continental system the financial burden was borne by the consumer, under the British system by the tax-payer. The consumer and the taxpayer are of course collectively the same person under different names, but the collective abstraction ignores widely differing patterns of consumption and of liability to taxation. It also ignores the interests of those Commonwealth countries (particularly the old white dominions) whose staple exports are non-tropical foodstuffs. To shift from the British to the continental system would therefore be a painful process.

It would not be an impossible step, however, and it was even argued that it would eventually be an inevitable one, whether or not Britain were to join the Common Market. But the Labour government showed small sign of recognising it in 1965. On the contrary, they proceeded with a review of agricultural prices under the existing system as if it were sacrosanct and eternal, though the figures which emerged gave a great deal of dissatisfaction to the farmers. The government were justified in taking this ultra-conservative attitude by a number of considerations. They did not wish to provoke avoidable trouble with either the Commonwealth or the British electorate (both of which were still in the main hostile to Britain's entry into Europe) or with the farmers (though in this case they were less successful). The disarray of the continental Six, which largely arose out of agricultural problems between themselves, was another good reason. But the substantial conclusion must be that, from whatever motives, the Labour government was unwilling to face the need for structural change in Britain's economic relations.

It is not to be suggested that the government was not active, and even vigorously active in a reformatory and radical sense. But its feverish activity in the first months of office was related only to the re-adjustment of the economy which it inherited, not to the fundamental solution of Britain's structural problems. Many of the earlier measures gave an impression of extemporisation: for instance, the 15% surcharge on imports and the three budgets introduced within twelve months. Others were radical only in the sense of being sharply re-distributive: such were the increases of pensions, redundancy payments and other welfare benefits, coupled with the heavy taxation to pay for them. Some were simply designed to make the mixed economy of private and public enterprise function more efficiently. There was a Statement of Intent by employers, Trade Unions, and government about implementing a wages and incomes policy; there was a Prices and Incomes Board to see that they did so, and the threat of legislation in case they did not; there was a National Plan drawn up by the new Department of Economic Affairs; there were new schemes of incentives in industrial investment and exports. But there was also a greatly accelerated rate of increase of wages and prices, and more stoppages of work by unofficial action than in any other year since the war.

Virtually none of the government's measures were socialist, however, in the sense of Clause 4 of the party constitution. A debate on the principle of nationalising the steel industry (May 1965) ended in a half-hearted vote in favour by the narrowest margin, gained mainly by a last-minute hint to dissident Labour back-benchers that some other course might be tried first; and in fact no further step was taken for the time being. There was a growing preference for more pragmatic, less doctrinaire methods of adjustment between private and public enterprise: for instance, a partnership between government, employers and unions to keep in being the Fairfield ship-building yard on the Clyde when it faced bankruptcy; or the proposal of the Plowden Report that the government should purchase a shareholding interest in the two major air-frame manufacturers; or the establishment of the Industrial Re-organisation Corporation, to promote mergers and rationalisation of lagging industries. Economic experts argued that it would have been preferable to let declining industries decline and to concentrate resources on growth-points; but on this issue the government's attitude was ambivalent.

Some decline it boldly permitted: in the coal industry, for instance, where the National Coal Board under Lord Robens (a former Labour Minister, appointed by the Conservative government) bluntly denounced increasing absenteeism and proposed to close another 150 pits. The logic of this decision was inescapable, especially at a time when the hopes of extracting natural gas in large quantities from under the North Sea were turning into practical certainties. On the railways, however, the government pursued a different course. It hastened the departure of the Conservative-appointed Chairman of the Railways Board, Dr Beeching; it held up closures wherever possible; and by yielding to the threat of a railway strike early in 1966, it failed to support the chairman of its own Prices and Incomes Board, Aubrey Jones (a former Conservative Minister, appointed by the Labour government). The best that could be said for these half-hearted policies was that they were dictated by political calculation (which is not to treat them with contempt) rather than by any long-range appreciation of the dramatic scale of Britain's problems.

The justification for the government's combination of opportunism and timidity in its initial period was that it was engaged in a desperate struggle to avert a major financial crisis, to restore foreign confidence in sterling, and to avoid having to devalue the pound (although some economists were urging the Chancellor to do just that). Whether the crisis was created by the government's own policies (as its critics said) or inherited from its predecessors (as its supporters said), is a question only relevant to the historian's judgement of its competence, not to the assessment of its other policies in 1965–66. The point is that all its other policies were dominated by the financial crisis. Foreign policy and defence policy, for example, might well have been much less subserviently harnessed to those of the USA if the government had not been so dependent on Washington for the rescue of sterling. Conceivably, though less probably, the same could be said of economic policy at home. In the event the government proved much less radical than it had promised, and that at a time when radical change was imperatively needed.

Paradoxically, however, this was not necessarily to be deplored, at least by the government's critics. For the kind of radicalism that was needed was not the same as the kind of radicalism that the government would probably have pursued if it had felt free to do so. An extension of socialism within the existing national framework might or might not be desirable on social and political grounds. But it could not have helped to solve problems which arose from the fact that the national framework was itself inadequate in scale and out of date. The Wilson government was in the position of a man seeking to make a Baby Austin do the job of a Rolls Royce. Not even the introduction of efficient spare parts from a borrowed Mini-Cooper could achieve the object. What was wanted was a new and larger vehicle, which could only be acquired by going into partnership with other drivers. There were few indications that the government had grasped the basic facts underlying this analogy.

There were few indications that the British public had grasped them, either. The general impression of energy and activity on the part of the government convinced the public that at last things were moving. Wilson's personality made a striking impact on television, where the Rhodesian crisis at the end of 1965 gave him ample opportunities of publicity; and the same crisis debarred Edward Heath, the new leader of the opposition, from competing with the Prime Minister, by virtue of the convention of national unity at a time of crisis overseas. Although there was a strong body of Conservative opinion which bitterly opposed the government's policy towards Rhodesia and resented Heath's reluctance to attack it more strongly, this was not an issue on which a responsible opposition could honourably seek popularity. The result was that the government gained support while the opposition lost support in the public opinion polls. The government's economic policy had the same effect: even if prices rose, at least the cost was being shared more equally. There was also a feeling of relief that it appeared to be possible, as the public had continued to hope throughout every post-war administration, to carry on with the British way of life at an acceptable standard of living without any radical upheaval, such as entering the Common Market. The long term might present a less favourable picture; but the long term was a long way off.

There was of course some awareness of unsolved problems. The attempt to establish a prices and incomes policy was visibly failing by the end of 1965, and the creation of a Ministry of Technology under Cousins and Snow was not a success. There were some contradictions of policy too glaring to be overlooked. One was the persistent opposition of the Transport and General Workers' Union (of which Cousins was still General Secretary on leave of absence) to the government's economic policy. Another was the conflict over immigration policy. Not only were the restrictions on coloured immigration proposed in the White Paper of August 1965 in sharp contrast to the pre-election policy of the Labour Party; they were also inconsistent with the National Plan published in the following month, which presupposed a shortage of at least 200,000 workers by 1970. But here again the public preferred the short-term political solution of keeping the immigrants out to the long-term economic solution of letting them in; and the government gave them what they wanted. Such was the simple formula by which Britain was governed at one of the gravest moments of her history.

It is a melancholy conclusion that what the British public seemed chiefly to want in 1966 was bread and circuses *plus* an illusion of greatness without effort. Those who dissented showed a growing tendency to emigrate. Those who agreed voted for the government most likely to supply their wants. It followed that the success of the Labour government was virtually inevitable when Wilson went to the country again after eighteen months in March 1966. And so it proved: his government increased its overall majority from three to nearly 100. Its sophisticated appearance of dynamism, combined with the conviction it conveyed that the British people could get along very well without any structural changes in their way of life, was pleasantly persuasive. Time might, as always, reverse both the trend and the mood. But time was not on Britain's side.

Conclusion

ONE DOES not have to be a Gaullist to believe that it is impossible for a great nation to sink into a permanent decline. One has only to accept—and this is the denial of Gaullism—that it is impossible to play a great role on a stage that is too narrow and flimsy to give the performer scope. For too long the British people had preferred the narrow stage, in a mood of nostalgic introspection, as if under the impression that they were still enjoying the 'splendid isolation' of 1900, or 'standing alone' as in 1940. Although crystal-gazing is no contribution to history, it is worth looking again at the close of the twenty-year period since the war, to see if there were any signs of the mood having passed. There were in fact some such signs in the seeds of time, but it was not possible to say with certainty which would ripen.

The signs were least difficult to discern in the material context. There was evident a growing realisation on the part of the Labour Party that it had been a mistake to turn its back so abruptly on Europe in its early days of office. They began to recognise the fact that as the major science-based industries—the spearhead of technological advance—became inevitably larger, more capital-intensive, and increasingly monopolistic within the national framework, both competition and collaboration must become international rather than national in character; and that whereas international competition meant chiefly competition with the USA and the Soviet Union, international collaboration could only be effective with powers of similar size and resources, which meant Europe. Big businesses were getting bigger, increasingly indifferent to national boundaries, and also increasingly disposed to accept guidance from the government. The crucial position of the aircraft and electronics industries in this scheme of things was belatedly recognised by the government in 1966. The closely related fact that the government was responsible for over half the scientific research in this country, including the employment of some 60%

of all British scientists and technologists, also meant that the field of competition was essentially international rather than exclusively domestic. Any government of the United Kingdom had to live with these facts, and therefore to look outward rather than inward. An inter-party consensus was at last beginning to emerge on the need to join Europe. The problem was not that the political leaders were unaware of the facts: it was rather whether the public would face them.

The short answer seemed to be in 1966 that the younger generation would, but a high proportion of the older generation would not. All groups and classes of society of course included both old and young: hence the uncertainty of the answer. If there were some signs that the British people in their various collective manifestations were beginning to look outward rather than inward, and forward rather than backward, there were not yet grounds for positive confidence. Nevertheless some points of encouragement could be detected in even the oldest and most hidebound sectors of the Establishment. The House of Lords admitted women and non-hereditary peers; the House of Commons admitted the need to modernise its proceedings and even contemplated televising them. The Stock Exchange opened a public gallery; even the Bank of England allowed a little information to seep out. The ancient universities of Oxford and Cambridge each conducted a personal inquest on itself, intended to promote reform. The Trade Union Congress not only recognised the need to put its house in order but even participated in a Royal Commission to that end. The Athenaeum Club admitted women and *The Times* inaugurated a women's page. First attempts were made, though strongly resisted, to merge the three armed services under a united Ministry of Defence, and to create a regional if not a national police force. None of these things was startlingly revolutionary in itself, but one had only to live in Britain through the last twenty years to appreciate that they might be the first cracks in the ice-cap.

Perhaps in the long run the most important area of innovation might prove to be religion. It was a common-place that Britain had largely ceased to be a Christian country; but as the

91

Russian Communists also found, the religious instinct—the belief that there is some spiritual purpose in life and the desire to discover it—dies much harder than institutionalised worship. Christian ministers were declining in numbers and in religious influence. Some were resorting to politics as a substitute, not without effect, though they acquired in the process some dubious allies. But others were pioneering in new directions which might in the long run be more profitable. Missionary activity was expanding rather than contracting. The enormous success of the *New English Bible*, of the Bishop of Woolwich's *Honest to God*, and of the exhibition of the Dead Sea Scrolls at the British Museum, were distinct but equally impressive portents. The good will generated by the Ecumenical Movement to unite the Christian Churches was profound, sincere and presumably continuing. The British had certainly not ceased to be a religious people even if the majority had ceased to be formally Christian. That was encouraging so far as it went, since a people without a religion is a people without a future. It was also encouraging that the Ecumenical Movement, like missionary activity, involved Britain in the world.

It is natural to relate to this trend the decline of faith in science. At the end of the war the prestige of scientists was immense, no doubt chiefly because they were the magicians who had released the energy of the atom. By the end of the nineteen-fifties their glamour seemed more questionable. People asked what was the point of the achievements for which they demanded so much money? The answer that space-satellites made it possible to spy effectively on the Soviet Union, to transmit television programmes across the Atlantic, and to cheapen telephone calls to Australia, seemed inadequate at a time when millions of Asians were starving. The infallibility of the scientist emerged badly tarnished when people learned from experience the unpleasant and even tragic side-effects of 'miracle drugs' such as cortisone, thalidomide and the contraceptive pill.

Scientists proved fallible even in their unique field of competence. For example, at an International Congress on Astronautics in 1951, it was recorded that not even the most optimistic expected piloted space-travel to be possible before the end of the century. If they were capable of a miscalculation by nearly forty years in their own field, why should their political judgement be trustworthy? It took time to learn the simple truth that a scientific education conferred no more political expertise than any other. Scientists and their admirers constantly lamented that there were so few scientists in the government—a justified criticism, but a criticism of the scientifically educated rather than of Parliament. The matter came to be seen in a more just perspective after the chief protagonist of this kind of criticism, Lord Snow, had been seen in office for a year or two.

Like all understandable reactions, however, the revulsion against science and the related acerbities of modern technology contained its own dangers. There was an ever-present temptation to relapse into the complacent self-admiration of a people whose past greatness could not be denied. We had pioneered so much in the way of social reform, material improvement, the arts and sciences: why should we not rest on our laurels? The answer was precisely because we had been the pioneers, and therefore everything produced in this country was out of date in comparison with the work of our imitators abroad. They were happy to give us the credit of pioneers while at the same time they took the bread out of our mouths. The credit was not enough, and we were slow to realise it. One reason why we were slow was because we had come through the Second World War exhausted but relatively intact. In contrast to our European neighbours, the destruction of this country was slight, and what was destroyed was, unfortunately, seldom what it would have been most useful to have scrapped. It must be admitted, however, that twenty years was a long time to take to learn these simple facts.

If a single crucial test were to be sought of the will and capacity for modernisation of the British people, it might well be found in the system of secondary education. The problem was social as well as educational. It was in the first place to eliminate a caste-system created by the existence of a fee-paying sector known as the 'public schools', which took little more than 5% of all the school-children in the country, but

93

enjoyed an entirely disproportionate influence. The second part of the problem was to mitigate the personal agonies of the method of selection in the state system at the age of 11, discriminating between those deserving to go to grammar schools and those fitted only for less exalted education. The third part of the problem was to do both these things not on grounds of doctrinaire egalitariansim but on educational grounds. After a year in office, the Labour government appeared less dedicated to the abolition of public schools and to the amalgamation of every type of school into 'comprehensives' than their official dogmas would have suggested. The problem was remitted, so far as comprehensive schools were concerned, to the local authorities, and so far as the public schools were concerned, to a commission under Sir John Newsom. But no easy solution was in sight; and a solution was imperatively needed if Britain was ever to play an effective part in the world again. Here is a key indicator to be watched.

A reasoned survey of the recent past history of the British people leads one to alternate from optimism to despair about their prospects in the rest of the twentieth century. It could not be denied that they had been moving through a long, slow decline for twenty years, living with the memories of 'their finest hour'. (It was significant that by far the most spectacular event of 1965 was the funeral of the author of those words.) The fact that the decline was long and slow was the most sinister thing about it. Britain was not becoming a poor country in the absolute sense, it goes without saying; and the internal disparities of wealth were probably less than in any other country in the world. But in terms of average wealth *per caput*, we have fallen to thirteenth place, from first place a century ago and second place even in our own lifetimes. Whether this trend, and many others related to it, can be reversed depends on a simple equation. Will the social forces which prevail be those which are directed forwards and outwards, or those which are directed backwards and inwards? There is no certain answer to be extracted from an historical survey. To end by preferring the favourable answer is only a mark of temperamental optimism.